ME AND JULIET

Me and Juliet

Music by RICHARD RODGERS

Book and Lyrics by

OSCAR HAMMERSTEIN, 2nd

RANDOM HOUSE · NEW YORK

To Dorothy
with love

ME AND JULIET *was first produced by Richard Rodgers and Oscar Hammerstein, 2nd, on March 28, 1953, at the Majestic Theatre, New York City, with the following cast:*

(In order of their appearance)

EMPLOYMENT IN THE THEATRE

GEORGE, 2nd Assistant Stage Manager,	Randy Hall
SIDNEY, Electrician,	Edwin Philips
JEANIE, Chorus Singer,	Isabel Bigley
HERBIE, Candy Counter Boy,	Jackie Kelk
CHRIS, Rehearsal Piano Player,	Barbara Carroll
MILTON, Drummer,	Herb Wasserman
STU, Bass Fiddle Player,	Joe Shulman
MICHAEL, A Chorus Boy,	Michael King
BOB, Electrician,	Mark Dawson
LARRY, Assistant Stage Manager,	Bill Hayes
MAC, Stage Manager,	Ray Walston
MONICA, Chorus Dancer,	Patty Ann Jackson
RUBY, Company Manager,	Joe Lautner
CHARLIE (Me), Featured Lead,	Arthur Maxwell
DARIO, Conductor,	George S. Irving
LILY (Juliet), Singing Principal,	Helena Scott
JIM (Don Juan), Principal Dancer,	Bob Fortier
SUSIE (Carmen), Principal Dancer,	Svetlana McLee
VOICE OF MR. HARRISON, Producer,	Henry Hamilton
VOICE OF MISS DAVENPORT, Choreographer,	Deborah Remsen
HILDA, An aspirant for a dancing part,	Norma Thornton
MARCIA, Another aspirant for a dancing part,	Thelma Tadlock
BETTY, Successor to Susie as Principal Dancer,	Joan McCracken
BUZZ, Principal Dancer,	Buzz Miller
RALPH, Alley Dancer,	Ralph Linn
MISS OXFORD, A Bit Player,	Gwen Harmon
SADIE, An Usher,	Francine Bond
MILDRED, Another Usher,	Lorraine Havercroft
A THEATRE PATRON	Barbara Lee Smith
ANOTHER THEATRE PATRON	Susan Lovell

ENSEMBLE: Company, Stage Crew, Audience.

DANCING ENSEMBLE: Francine Bond, Betty Buday, Penny Ann Green, Lorraine Havercroft, Patty Ann Jackson, Helene Keller, Lucia Lambert, Harriet Leigh, Sonya Lindgren, Elizabeth Logue, Shirley MacLaine, Cheryl Parker, Dorothy Silverherz, Thelma Tadlock, Norma Thornton, Janyce Ann Wagner, Rosemary Williams.

Lance Avant, Grant Delaney, John George, Jack Konzal, Ralph Linn, Eddie Pfeiffer, Augustine Rodriguez, Bob St. Clair, Bill Weber.

SINGING ENSEMBLE: Adele Castle, Gwen Harmon, Susan Lovell, Theresa Mari, Georgia Reed, Deborah Remsen, Thelma Scott, Barbara Lee Smith.

Jack Drummond, John Ford, Henry Hamilton, Richard Hermany, Warren Kemmerling, Michael King, Larry Laurence, Jack Rains.

Production directed by George Abbott

Dances and musical numbers staged by Robert Alton

Scenery and lighting by Jo Mielziner

Costumes designed by Irene Sharaff

SCENES

The entire action takes place in the theatre in which *Me and Juliet* is currently playing.

ACT ONE

ACT TWO

MUSICAL NUMBERS

ACT ONE

1. (a) A Very Special Day   Jeanie and Trio
   (b) That's the Way It Happens   Jeanie and Trio
2. Reprise: That's the Way It Happens   Larry
3. Dance Impromptu   Chorus, George and Trio
4. Overture to *Me and Juliet*   Dario and Orchestra
5. Opening of *Me and Juliet*   Lily, Jim, Susie and Charlie
6. Marriage Type Love   Charlie, Lily and Singers
7. Keep It Gay   Bob, Jim and Chorus
8. Reprise: Keep It Gay   Betty and Buzz
9. The Big, Black Giant   Larry
10. No Other Love   Jeanie and Larry
11. Dance   Ralph, Francine and Elizabeth
12. Reprise: The Big, Black Giant   Ruby
13. It's Me   Betty and Jeanie
14. First Act Finale of *Me and Juliet*   Lily, Betty, Charlie, Jim, Jeanie and Chorus

ACT TWO

1. Intermission Talk   Herbie and Chorus
2. It Feels Good   Bob
3. Sequence in Second Act of *Me and Juliet*:
   We Deserve Each Other   Betty, Jim and Dancers
4. I'm Your Girl   Jeanie and Larry
5. Second Act Finale of *Me and Juliet*   Charlie, Lily, Betty, Jim and Chorus
6. Finale of Our Play   Entire Company

ACT ONE

ACT ONE

Scene I

The curtain rises on a bare stage. The proscenium arch is off center, so that we see the off-stage area on the right. In the foreground the light bridge is lowered half way to the floor. A rehearsal piano is set, stage left; the stage manager's desk, stage right.

JEANIE is playing the piano. GEORGE, the assistant stage manager, enters.

GEORGE

Half hour! Half hour!

BOY
(Entering left)

Hi, George!
(SIDNEY, the electrician, enters, carrying a lamp.)

SIDNEY

How about some lights!

GEORGE
(Calling off stage)

Hey, Louis! Give us some lights!

3

ME AND JULIET

VOICE
VOICE

(*Off stage*)

Okay!

(*The lights come on.*)

GEORGE

Half hour! Half hour!
(*He exits.* SIDNEY *goes to a ladder that stands under the light bridge and carries the lamp up the ladder.* MILTON, *the drummer, has entered to set his drums above the piano.* JEANIE *rises from piano, striking keys with palms of her hands in a discordant bang.*)

MILTON

(*Looking at* JEANIE)
That sounds kinda modern.
(*Exits.*)

JEANIE

(*Coming down to* SIDNEY)
I've been stood up. Bob told me he was coming in early.

SIDNEY

He told me he was coming early too. He's supposed to be here right now helping me. . . . Jeanie, how long have you been going with Bob?

JEANIE

Since the show opened—about six months.

4

SIDNEY

This the first time he stood you up?

JEANIE

No.

SIDNEY

Don't you ever get sore at him?

JEANIE

Sure I do. (*Smiling resignedly*) But he's always so sorry when he does anything wrong. He's like a kid.

SIDNEY

Yeah. He's cute.

JEANIE

You don't like Bob, do you?

SIDNEY

I like him all right. I'm up on this bridge with him all the time. We have a lot of laughs together. If that's all you want out of him he's fine. But if anybody gets an idea she can make him into something better than he is, she's letting herself in for something. That's all I gotta say. . . . Excuse me for butting in.

JEANIE

Oh, don't apologize, I get a lot of advice about Bob from everybody.

(She saunters away, toward the Stage Manager's desk. HERBIE *enters with his "Trio,"* CHRIS, *a piano player;* STU, *a bass fiddler; and* MILTON, *the drummer.)*

HERBIE

Come on kids it'll be curtain time before you know it. Come on, get going! Know what we're doing, Sidney? We're getting up a Trio. (HERBIE *turns to the* TRIO, *who have started playing*) That's it kids. (*To* SIDNEY) We're going on Arthur Godfrey's Talent Scouts.

SIDNEY

You going to be the Scout?

HERBIE

Sure. Can you see me sitting up there at the desk next to Arthur Godfrey?

SIDNEY

Yeh. I can hear you too. He'll ask you where you come from and you'll say Brooklyn and everybody'll clap.
(GEORGE *comes back and meets two girls and a boy as they enter and cross the stage.*)

GIRL

Hi ya, George. Going to give us a little music on your whistle?

GEORGE

Better get made up first.

GIRL

We'll put on our smocks.

2ND GIRL

On the way down to get our costumes . . .

GEORGE

O.K.

> (*They exit.* JEANIE *is now seated at the Stage Manager's desk. Lost in her own thoughts, she sighs to herself.*)

JEANIE

Oh, dear!
> (*She sings:*)

Am I building something up
That really isn't there?
Do I make a big romance
Of a small affair?
Should I be more practical
As friends would have me be?
. . . Being practical is very hard for me.

I wake up each morning
With a feeling in my heart
That today will be a very special day.

I keep right on clinging
To that feeling in my heart
Till the winds of evening blow my dreams away.
Later on, at bedtime,
When my world has come apart
And I'm in my far from fancy negligee—
With a piece of toast to munch
And a nice hot cup of tea,
I begin to have a hunch
That tomorrow's going to be
A very special day for me.

> (*Voices in* JEANIE's *mind.*)

Jeanie, would you get sore if I offered some advice?
You can do better than him, Jeanie.
Why an electrician?
How'd you happen to tie up with a guy like that?
How does a thing like that start?

JEANIE

How does it start?
> (*She sings:*)

You're a girl from Chicago
On the road with a show—
Not a soul in New Haven
You can say you know.

> You wish you were a mile or so from Michigan Lake,
> Home with your mother and a T-bone steak.

Then along comes a fellow
With a smile like a kid,
And he gets your attention
With a timely bid.

He says he knows a bistro where they give you a break
With French fried potatoes and a T-Bone steak!
You are shy and uncertain
But he pleads and you yield,
And you don't have an inkling
That you're signed and sealed
    By merely telling someone you'd be glad to partake
    Of French fried potatoes and a T-Bone steak.
       That's the way it happens,
       That's the way it happens,
       That's the way it happened to me!
(JEANIE *exits. Several boys and girls enter.*)

BOY

Hey, did you see this in Variety? (*Reading*) "Musical pays off. Backers of *Me and Juliet* out of red and due to collect plenty on unconventional dance opera."

BOB
(*Entering*)

Hi, Sidney!

SIDNEY

Well!

BOB

Am I late?

SIDNEY

Yes, you're late.

9

BOB

I just ran into a guy I knew.

SIDNEY

That was nice.

BOB

You're not sore, are you, angel face?
(*He musses* SIDNEY's *hair up*)

SIDNEY

Get to work on that cable. We haven't got much time. (BOB *starts to work on a cable that is coiled on the floor near the stepladder. More of the* COMPANY *enter*) Jeanie was here just now.

BOB

Why didn't she wait for me? (SIDNEY *gives him a sarcastic look*) Was she sore? (SIDNEY *shrugs his shoulders*) Guess I'll have to talk my way out of it, huh? (*He chuckles*) She's a sweet kid.

SIDNEY

(*With studied casualness*)
Ever think you'd like to marry Jeanie?

BOB

Me? Not on your life! . . . I know *too many* guys who got hooked. You know what happens soon's you get married? Right away the dame's got to go to the dentist and get all

her teeth fixed. You get a bill for three hundred bucks. That's
only the beginning . . .

SIDNEY

(*Getting angry on* JEANIE's *behalf*)
Ah, she wouldn't have you anyway. I'm surprised she even
talks to you. (*A puzzled expression crosses* BOB's *face. He's
not quite sure whether* SIDNEY *is kidding or not*) One of the
best-lookin' babes in the show. You'd think she could get
something better'n a baboon like you. (BOB *comes behind*
SIDNEY *and grabs him by the collar of his shirt, and by the
seat of his trousers, and lifts him up so that he's nearly clear
of the ground. Everyone on stage stands still and silent,
worried and fascinated, witnessing a big man bullying a little
man*) Hey, what are you doing? Cut it out, Bob! I got the
lens in my hand! Want me to break it? I was only kiddin'.
Cut it out, I tell you! You damn fool!

BOB

Who's a damn fool?
(BOB, *still holding* SIDNEY's *trousers with one hand,
garrotes him with the other arm.*)

SIDNEY

(*His voice muffled, choking*)
You're hurting me! (BOB *releases him*) What the hell's the
matter with you, anyway? (BOB *walks away, roaring with
laughter. More of the* COMPANY *enter, sense something
wrong*) You're a cute kid! Funny as hell! (BOB *laughs even*

11

louder) What's the matter with you? You getting like you used to be! (BOB *stops laughing suddenly.*)

BOB

What's that?

> (JEANIE *enters dressed like the other girls in the knee-length smock that is worn before they go downstairs to put on their costumes. She remains upstage, unseen by the others.*)

SIDNEY

(*Staring back at* BOB *with the reckless courage of panic*) I said . . .

BOB

I heard what you said. (*He walks slowly over to* SIDNEY *and stands in front of him*) And don't ever say that again. (*Raising his voice to a shout*) You hear? (*Lowering his voice again*) Don't you ever . . . I'm not like I used to be—and it's damn lucky for you I'm not. (*He stands scowling down at* SIDNEY *as if not quite sure whether he will throttle him or not. Then he becomes conscious of* JEANIE's *presence. Embarrassed, he switches to his other self—the big charm boy*) Hello, Jeanie . . . (*A nervous laugh*) What do you know about this guy Sidney? Trying to kid me—said you were sore because I got here late. (*He walks over to her*) You're not sore, are you, kid?

JEANIE
(*Uncertainly*)

No.

ME AND JULIET

(*The* TRIO *start to play again. A few of the boys and girls start to slip easily into some light jazz steps, but this is all done upstage of the piano.*)

BOB

Know what made me late? I was lookin' at that piano.
(JEANIE *stops and turns slowly, as if unable to resist talking about the piano.*)

JEANIE

The one I told you about?

BOB

Yeh. On Fifty-seventh Street. The little one.
(*Pause.*)

JEANIE

Did you like it?

BOB

Sure did. Wish I could buy it for you. Maybe by Christmas I can save enough for a down payment, huh?
(*Pause.*)

JEANIE

What were you and Sidney fighting about?

BOB

We weren't fighting. We were just clowning. Weren't we, Sid?

13

SIDNEY

(*Working on his lamp*)

Yeh. Just clowning.

HERBIE

(*Referring to the music his* TRIO *is making*)

Ain't that crazy!

BOB

Come here. I want to tell you something.
(*He grabs* JEANIE, *lifts her onto Stage Manager's desk, and starts to whisper to her.*)

LARRY

(*Entering*)

Hey, Sidney, we've got to get this bridge out of the way. People will be coming in and knocking the lamps off—their angles.
(*He stops in the middle of his sentence because he has looked over and seen* JEANIE *sitting on the desk talking to* BOB.)

HERBIE

(*Coming over to him*)

Hi, Larry. Did you hear what I'm going to do for these kids? I'm going to get them a chance with Arthur Godfrey. When I get on the air, would you like me to give you a plug? Like I can say we got an assistant stage manager who's one great guy?

ME AND JULIET

LARRY

Excuse me a minute, Herbie. (*He goes over to the desk*) Bob. I'm afraid I've got to get at my desk. I've got some work.

BOB

Okay. This is your desk. (*Picking up* JEANIE) And this is my girl. (BOB *exits, carrying* JEANIE *off with him.*)
(*The boys and girls start to dance softly to the* TRIO's *music. The lights come down on the dancers who group around the piano, swaying in rhythm.* LARRY, *at his desk, starts to think back on the recent past, just as* JEANIE *did when she sat there a few minutes ago.*)

LARRY

(*Singing*)

You're a guy in New Haven on the road with a show.
There's a girl in the company that you hardly know.
    You watch her and you wonder if she'd like to partake
    Of French fried potatoes and a T-Bone steak.
    (*He looks off where* BOB *carried* JEANIE)
Then along comes a fellow who is quicker than you,
And he does what you thought that you would like to do—
    He takes her to a bistro where they give you a break
    With French fried potatoes and a T-Bone steak.
Now you see them together and you know in your heart
That you lost what you wanted at the very start,
    Because you didn't ask her if she'd like to partake
    Of French fried potatoes and a T-Bone steak!

15

That's the way it happens,
That's the way it happens,
That's the way it happened to me.

SIDNEY

(Shouting up to the flies)
Hey, Ernie! Take the bridge up a little.
> *(The spot fades on* LARRY *and the lights come up on the dancing group. The music and dancing both get hot now.* GEORGE, *the assistant stage manager, augments the* TRIO *with his tin whistle, and maintaining a spontaneous and impromptu spirit, the dance builds up to a big climax and stops. After applause it is started again, and after about sixteen measures* MAC *enters. As they see him, the dancers stop and so do the musicians.* MAC *stands in the center of the stage looking from one to another. He is obviously respected as a disciplinarian. After he has achieved a few seconds of awed silence he turns slowly and speaks to* LARRY *quietly.)*

MAC

Two minutes after, Larry!

LARRY

(Feeling guilty like the rest)
Oh . . . er . . . George, see if they're all signed in.

GEORGE

(Making the call as he crosses the stage and exits)
Fifteen minutes! Fifteen minutes!

MAC

(*Meanwhile* MAC *turns to the rest of the company who are melting away very quickly. He calls to the last girl going out. She is the color of a cooked lobster*)

Monica! (MONICA *turns and tries to look casual*) I see you've been down to the beach.

MONICA

(*Assuming gay and girlish innocence*)
How do you like my sunburn?

MAC

Great! Just dandy. Best way I know to take the audience's mind off a play. (*She opens her mouth to answer but closes it again*) Sometimes a girl dances so much better than all the others that she stands out like a sore thumb. You've got a different way. You try to *look* like a sore thumb! (*She looks down at herself to check*) Go and get dressed. (MONICA *crosses left to some girls, one of whom starts to put her hand on* MONICA'S *shoulder.*)

MONICA

Ouch!
(*They exit down left.* MAC *turns to* LARRY.)

MAC

Let's have a look at the report. (LARRY *hands it to him. He starts to read it*) We ran three minutes longer last night.

17

LARRY

Yes. Lost one minute on intermission.
>   (RUBY, *the company manager, enters.*)

RUBY

Herbie, I'm only the company manager, but . . .

HERBIE
>   (*To* RUBY)

Hey, Ruby, have you heard, I'm sponsoring an act on the Arthur Godfrey show?

RUBY

If Mr. Shubert drops in and sees nobody behind your candy counter, who's going to sponsor *you?*

HERBIE

Gosh! I didn't know it was so late.
>   (*He exits.* RUBY *turns and exits on the other side. During the ensuing scene the crew are setting up the scenery and props for the first scene of* Me and Juliet.)

MAC

>   (*His eyes still on the stage manager's report, pretending to read it while he speaks*)

That was quite a clambake going on when I came in here.

18

LARRY

I guess I should have stopped it. They were all having such a good time that I . . .

MAC

Well, let them have a good time after the show. I don't care if . . .

GIRL

(*Running across stage*)
I'm awfully sorry, the traffic was terrible!
(LARRY *becomes conscious that* MAC *has looked up from the report and is studying him.*)

LARRY

I suppose you're thinking I'll never make a good stage manager.

MAC

(*After a pause*)
Is that what you want to be?

LARRY

Why, yes. I guess so. Sure.

MAC

What you really want to be is a director, isn't it?

LARRY

Yes, but I ought to learn to run a stage first.

19

MAC

Not necessarily. Lots of good directors were lousy stage managers. Josh Logan was a lousy stage manager.

LARRY

That's encouraging.

MAC

Stage managing is a special kind of job, like directing or acting or anything else. The stage manager is like the mayor of a small town. He's got to . . .

CHARLIE

(*Shouting off stage*)

Mac! (*Hearing the note in* CHARLIE'S *voice,* MAC *winces.* CHARLIE *enters left in a dressing gown and crosses to them, fuming*) Mac, I don't want to pull any corny temperament . . . (*He picks up a chair by the desk and bangs it on the floor*) But has an actor got the right to have the audience hear him when he sings? . . . Does the audience come to hear him? (*He starts to raise his voice*) —or do they come to hear a lot of trombones and drums. Just tell me! I want to know! (*He is now screeching*) That idiot! That conductor!

MAC

I'll talk to Dario.

CHARLIE

Well, damn it, if you don't . . .

ME AND JULIET

LARRY

Here's Dario. Take it easy.

(*Following his eyes,* MAC *and* CHARLIE *turn and see* DARIO, *who has just entered left. He is wearing a dinner coat and carries a small square cardboard box, which he puts on the piano. During the ensuing dialogue he opens it.*)

CHARLIE

(*Lowering his voice*)

Well, tell him.

MAC

I'll tell him.

CHARLIE

(*Still whispering, but through his teeth*)

Because if he does it to me again tonight, I'm going downstairs and wait outside the pit, and when he comes out I'm going to punch him right in the nose.

MAC

I'll tell him.

(CHARLIE *turns and crosses the stage. As he passes him,* DARIO *looks up.*)

DARIO

(*He is just taking a gardenia out of the box*)

Good evening, Charlie.

CHARLIE

(*With friendly heartiness*)

Hi ya, Dario baby!

(CHARLIE *exits,* MAC'S *eyes following him off as he muses.*)

MAC

Lovable Charlie Clay! Audiences adore him—they say he's got a wistful quality.

LARRY

(*Nodding toward* DARIO)

Is it true that Dario is leaving the show?

MAC

He *thinks* he's leaving. But he's the best conductor in town and I'm not going to let him go.

LARRY

How're you going to get him to stay if he doesn't want to?

MAC

I got a gimmick. (*Looking across speculatively at* DARIO *who has taken a letter from the box and is reading it*) See that letter he's reading? It's from a dame who signs herself "the gardenia lady"—says she's crazy about him, and that she'll be somewhere in the audience tonight.

LARRY

How do you know what's in the letter?

MAC

I wrote it. (DARIO *having read the letter, folds it tenderly and puts it in his breast pocket. With a soulful smile he puts the gardenia in his lapel*) I'm going to send him one every night. I figure he won't leave the show till he finds out who the dame is.

(*By this time, Scene One of* Me and Juliet *has been set. It is off center at the moment—and the* COMPANY *are drifting onto the stage and taking their places. The dancers, as usual, are stretching and limbering up.*)

DARIO

(*Crossing to* MAC *and* LARRY, *walking on a cloud*)
Good evening, gentlemen. Is it time for me to go in yet?

MAC

Just about. (DARIO *turns and starts to exit, humming happily.* MAC *calls to him*) Oh, Dario! (DARIO *turns*) Charlie says . . .

DARIO

I know! I am drowning him out! Every night the same. (*Starting to work himself up into a temper something like* CHARLIE'S) Tell him for me that thirty men in an orchestra can play no quieter!

MAC

Well, he's got a cold. Got a bum throat.

DARIO

(Raising his voice)

He was born with a bum throat. That man is my only reason for leaving the show. You know that!

MAC

(Pointing at the gardenia, tactfully changing the subject)
No carnation tonight?

DARIO

(Immediately brought back to heaven, looking down at his lapel)

No. I thought I would wear a gardenia tonight.
> *(He smiles with serene contentment.* GEORGE *crosses the stage to* MAC.*)*

GEORGE

O.K., Mac, I've sent the men in.

DARIO

Good. I shall go down. Funny thing. I just feel like playing the show tonight.
> *(He turns and starts to sing happily as he exits through the wings.)*

MAC

(To LARRY*)*

I think this is going to work. I want to go out front for the overture. Want to see what happens when Dario goes into the orchestra pit. I bet he'll get dizzy looking around for that dame.

> (MAC *starts off. More of the company keep coming on.* LILY, *who plays "Juliet," calls after him.*)

LILY

(Entering)

Oh, Mac. I've arranged with the office to take my vacation in August.

MAC

(Starts to exit)

Okay, Lily. Have a good time. *(Sees two girls sitting on chairs)* Get up off those costumes! *(Exits.)*

LARRY

(Calling to JEANIE, *who has come on with the others)*

Jeanie! *(He walks over to her)* I wanted to ask you something. When Lily takes her vacation in August, her understudy will have to go on. *(*JEANIE *looks at him steadily, waiting for him to finish his story. This disconcerts* LARRY *and he stutters and stumbles a bit)* You know, in the summertime, when understudies cover principals, we've got to get other understudies to—er—cover *them.*

JEANIE

Gee, Larry, I don't think I'd even have the nerve to go on. I don't want to be an actress. The only reason I tried to get in this show was because the pay was good.

LARRY

The pay'll be fifteen dollars a week more if you make second understudy.

JEANIE

Me play Juliet! I don't think I'm the Juliet type.

LARRY

I think you are . . . Help you buy that piano.

JEANIE

How did you know?

LARRY

About the piano? You told me once. You said you knew just where you'd put it—between two windows in your room.

JEANIE

Imagine your remembering that!
(*LARRY goes to his desk and calls into microphone.*)

LARRY

Overture! (*CHARLIE has come on and joined a group of girls. They are heard laughing at one of his jokes*) Everybody in first scene—places on stage!

SIDNEY

(*Calling up to the fly floor*)
Ernie, let her in!
(*The light bridge is lowered.*)

JEANIE

I can't understand how that happened to stick in your mind—about me saving up for a piano. How did you happen to remember that?

LARRY

I remembered it. Thought about it often.

BOB

(*Entering*)

Here we go, kid.

(*He gives* JEANIE *a proprietary slap and mounts the light bridge with* SIDNEY.)

LARRY

(*Into microphone*)

Overture! Everybody in first scene! Overture!

A BOY

(*Walking up to a girl*)

Can I have some of your mascara?

GIRL

Sure.

(*He takes some mascara off her eyelash, between his thumb and forefinger.*)

27

BOY

Got a hole in my tights.

> (*The boy rubs the black mascara on his leg to cover up the hole. This is all done with the laconic resourcefulness of professionals.*)

SIDNEY

> (*On bridge with* BOB, *calling up to fly floor*)

Take it away!

> (*The bridge is raised slowly. The* Me and Juliet *curtain is lowered in front of it, but it is transparent while the lights remain on behind it. Therefore you can see the bridge being raised with its colored lights glowing. On the stage the singers start to warm up with scales and exercises. The dancers limber up and stretch.* JEANIE *waves to* BOB *as the bridge goes up and then she looks over at* LARRY. *As the curtain hits the stage the lights are taken off behind it and it is no longer transparent.*)

Scene II

The orchestra pit.

The lights flood the show-curtain of Me and Juliet. *Then a spot hits* DARIO *entering the pit. As he mounts the stand he gazes around the audience, obviously trying to spot the lady of the gardenia. He taps the stand and starts the overture.*

OVERTURE—DARIO AND ORCHESTRA

For a while he concentrates on the music. Then, at a sentimental part, he turns around again and takes a chance that the lady of the gardenia is watching him. He lowers his nose and smells his gardenia passionately. He goes back to conducting, then as the orchestra starts to build to its climax, he looks around to make sure she is watching his magnificent gyrations. After he brings his baton down on the last beat of the overture, he turns and takes a bow and takes advantage of the bowing to look again for his "lady of the gardenia" and to blow a kiss at her, wherever she may be. Then he turns, lifts his baton, and brings it down to start the short prelude which will bring the curtain up on Me and Juliet.

SCENE III

The curtain rises on a dark stage. A pin spot hits JULIET, *who stands on a balcony. Below the balcony are her hand-maidens, who are as yet not seen, but now their voices are heard.*

VOICES

Where is this?

JULIET

It doesn't matter.
The scene of the play
Is neither here nor there.
All the things
About to happen
Are things that are always happening everywhere.

VOICES

When is this?

JULIET

It doesn't matter.
The time of the play
Is neither now nor then.
Every year
The world is changing—

But women remain the same—
>(*A spot hits* CARMEN)
And so do men!
>(*A spot hits* DON JUAN. *He is surrounded by girls.*)

VOICES

Who are they?
>(*A spot hits* ME.)

ME

They are the most important people in my life.

VOICES

Who are you?

ME

I? I am ME.
I am an ordinary character,
With an extraordinary interest in myself.
My own conception of ME—
>(*He looks at his clothes*)
Is—er—idealized.
The things that happen to ME seem remarkable.
The people I know—
Well, look at them!
>(*Indicating* DON JUAN)
This man, here, is my boss.
His name is Emil Phlugfelder.
But he has so many girls chasing him
That I call him DON JUAN.

(DON JUAN *starts to move, slowly, rhythmically. The*
GIRLS *dance with him.* ME *watches him enviously. After*
DON JUAN *exits with the girls,* ME *looks up at* JULIET,
then comes downstage and explains her to the audi-
ence.)

On the mezzanine floor
Of the place where I work
There's a girl—
One of the file clerks.

(*He turns toward* JULIET)
I look up from my desk
And there she is, on the balcony.
I always see her in a kind of glow.
To me, she is—JULIET!
She's the girl I'm going to marry.

(*Walking toward* CARMEN)
This one is a girl
I am *not* going to marry . . .
But she *bothers* me.
I see her everywhere—
In the subway, in the park, on the beach.
I call her—CARMEN.

(CARMEN *dances toward him. He backs away but is*
fascinated by her. Then there is practically a stam-
pede of men rushing on from the left toward CARMEN.
ME *steps aside and* CARMEN *dances with the men. As*
she exits with them she looks back temptingly at ME,
who looks after her a bit wistfully. Then ME *turns*
away and comes down toward the audience.)

Now you know them all,

The characters who will shape my life.
But this one—
    (*Indicating* JULIET)
My life didn't really begin
Till I met her.
I'll never forget our first date.
We sat on a park bench and fed the pigeons!
Ah, Juliet!
Look at her!
So young, so in need of protection.
As soon as you see a girl like that,
You want to marry her,
So that you can protect her
From all the men
Who want to protect her from you!
    (*He looks back at her*)
She makes me think of gentle and beautiful things:
Sunlit meadows, the laughter of children—
Juliet!
    (*She is coming down to him. He turns to audience*)
When she speaks, it is like the faint echo
Of far-off bells on a misty morning.
    (*He turns back to* JULIET)
Speak to me, Juliet!

JULIET

(*In a voice that sounds like a misty morning, but with no
bells in it*)
    Hi!
    (*He sighs ecstatically.*)

ME AND JULIET

(He sings)

When first I laid my longing eyes on you
I saw my future shining in your face,
And when you smiled and murmured "Howd'you do?"
The room became a dream-enchanted place.

  The chandeliers were shooting stars,
  The drums and horns and soft guitars
  Were sounding more like nightingales,
  The window curtains blew like sails,
  And I was floating just above the floor,
  Feeling slightly taller than before.

Out of nowhere
Came the feeling,
Knew the feeling—
  Marriage type love.
We were dancing
And your eyelash
Blinked on my lash—
  Marriage type love!
We made a date, couldn't wait
  For my day off.
Now it's a thing with a ring
  For the pay-off!
I'm your pigeon,
Through with roaming,
I am homing
  To marriage type love and you.

    *(The chorus joins them in singing. As the curtain
    comes down on this prologue to* Me and Juliet, CHAR-
    LIE *as* ME *and* LILY *as* JULIET *step forward so that the*

ME AND JULIET

curtain is behind them. They sing an encore refrain during which DARIO *makes the orchestra play very loudly and drown* CHARLIE *out every time he sings. When* JULIET *sings he plays softly. As the refrain is ended* JULIET *blows a kiss to* DARIO *as she exits and* CHARLIE, *infuriated, mutters something which if you can read lips is very insulting indeed. Scowling at* DARIO *he makes his exit.)*

Scene IV

The Light Bridge.
BOB *and* SIDNEY *are busily changing colors in their lamps.*

SIDNEY
(Continuing an argument)
All right, so I'm stupid! I still say I don't know what the hell it's about . . . First thing that happens, a dame comes out and tells the audience the scene is no place and the time is any time at all. If they don't know where the hell they are, how are the audience going to know?

BOB
It's symbolic. This guy they call "Me"—he's the kind that wants a wife and a couple of kids and a little house somewhere, Flushing or some place like that.

SIDNEY
Flushing, huh? I don't live so far from there.

BOB
That's what I mean.

SIDNEY
You mean I'm like him?

36

BOB

In a general way.

SIDNEY

(*Derisively*)

Ah, go on! Do you think I'd be acting like he's acting now? Look at him down there! Sitting on a park bench! That Carmen giving him the business and him looking like a scared rabbit. Look at her! Rollin' her eyes at him.

BOB

Boy, she's rolling everything! You can see good from up here . . . Did y'ever think what fun it'd be to stand up here and drop sandbags on the actors? Pick 'em off one by one!

SIDNEY

Look at that guy now! Why don't he give in to that Carmen dame?

BOB

He's got the other one on his mind. Don't you see she's in a vision back there. He sees Juliet in his dreams while that Carmen dame is trying to make him. When a guy makes up his mind to marry, he doesn't want to look at any outside stuff—for a while. Didn't you feel like that before you got married? (SIDNEY *thinks*) Well, didn't you?

SIDNEY

I'm just trying to remember. The way I proposed to Josephine was kinda funny. All her family were there, her mother and her father and three brothers. And the oldest

37

brother said, "When are you kids going to get married?" And everybody looked at me, and I said, "Oh, whenever Josephine will have me." You know, I was kinda half joking . . . Five minutes later all the neighbors came in and we were having drinks and that's what they called announcing the engagement.

BOB

Well, you loved her, didn't you?

SIDNEY

Sure I loved her.

BOB

So you see, the other dames couldn't tempt you, could they?

SIDNEY

How do I know? Nobody tried! Nobody like that Carmen down there.

(BOB *looks down. The refrain of "Keep It Gay" is being played.*)

BOB

This Don Juan feller, he's more like me. We like a good time.

SIDNEY

Aw, so do I like a good time.

BOB

(*Laughing*)

Sure you do. You *like* it, but you don't *get* it.

(BOB *sings with the music*)

"Let it sing like a nightingale in May,
Keep it Gay."

SIDNEY

(*In a loud whisper*)
Sh! They'll hear you down there!

BOB

They can't hear me.
    (*Singing*)
"Take it easy and enjoy it while you take it!"

SIDNEY

If you like singing so much why don't you get a job as an
actor?

BOB

I bet I could play the part better than the mug who's play-
ing it now.
    (*He sings*)
When a girl would meet Don Juan
She'd get goofy for the Don.
Like a snake who meets a mongoose
That young lady was a gone goose.
Any time a girl would say:
"Shall we name a wedding day?"
Juan would try another gambit
(He liked weddings not a damn bit).
He would gaze into the lady's eye,
Strumming his guitar to stall for time.

39

Then he'd make his usual reply—
That old reliable Andalusian rhyme:
> Keep it gay,
> Keep it light,
> Keep it fresh,
> Keep it fair.
> Let it bloom
> Ev'ry night,
> Give it room,
> Give it air!
> Keep your love a lovely dream and never wake it.
> Make it happy and be happy as you make it!
> Let it sing
> Like a nightin-
> gale in May,
> Keep it gay.
> Keep it free
> Or you'll frighten
> It away.
> Take it easy and enjoy it while you take it!
> Keep it gay,
> Keep it gay,
> Keep it gay!

> (*The lights go out on* SIDNEY *and* BOB *and immediately come up on the stage below where* DON JUAN *and the girls are dancing this same number in* Me and Juliet. *At a certain point in the dance the lights go out and a few seconds later come up, finding* DON JUAN *and the chorus in the same pose, only they are now in practice clothes, rehearsing the number. This is the beginning of the next scene.*)

Scene V

The bare stage.

CHRIS *is playing the piano for rehearsal over at the right side of the stage.* RUBY *leans on the piano, just sort of "hanging around, watching things."* LARRY *stands against the proscenium. Upstage are flats and drops from the production of* Me and Juliet. *Around the traveler curtains, on either side, are wooden rails to protect them, and "pants" of burlap around them, as there were in Scene I.*

After the dance MAC'S *voice can be heard from the front of the house.*

MAC'S VOICE

All right! All right! That was fine! Now we've got it back to the way we had it!

> (*The* COMPANY *stand, sit and lie on the stage, panting heavily, looking out front, listening to* MAC, *as if he were making a speech from about the tenth row. They seem faintly embarrassed, as all groups do when listening to a speech from a stage manager or producer.*)

I know it's no fun rehearsing on a hot day in June, but it's also no fun to be out of a job on a cold day in February, and that's what'll happen to all of us if we don't keep these performances up. O.K. That's all. Thank you.

> (*The group breaks up and drifts off stage, some quickly, others slowly.* SIDNEY *comes down to the very*

*edge of the stage and peers out into the dark audi-
torium.)*

SIDNEY

Hey, Mac! Can I have the stage now?

MAC'S VOICE

(From the front)
Not right away. We've got replacement auditions for the
part of Carmen. You can have it in about twenty minutes.

LARRY

(Coming down quickly)
I've got an understudy call right after the audition.

SIDNEY

Then when the hell am I going to get a chance to change
my color frames? *(Talking out to* MAC*)* All the colors are
faded. You were complaining last night.

MAC'S VOICE

Who are you rehearsing, Larry?

LARRY

Second understudy for Juliet. I'm trying out Jeanie.
(There is a pause.)

42

ME AND JULIET

MAC'S VOICE

Oh . . . Well, hold it a minute. I'll come up on stage and we'll talk it over.

(LARRY *turns to* SIDNEY, *in the manner of one making a retreat.*)

LARRY

I think we can work it out all right, Sidney. I'll rehearse downstage here, if you'll try not to make a lot of noise.

SIDNEY

(*Smiling as if he knows a secret*)
I'll be as quiet as a little mouse, chum. I wouldn't interfere with your—rehearsal—for anything in the world.

(SIDNEY *exits across the other side of the stage.*)

CHRIS

(*To* RUBY)
What's that about replacement auditions for Carmen?

RUBY

We've got to get a new one. Susie's leaving. She's going to have a baby.

CHRIS

Susie?

RUBY

Ask Susie's husband.

GIRL

Jim?

43

JIM

Yes, I am—I mean she is.

MAC

(*Entering, making a general announcement to all the stragglers*)
Clear the stage! We're having auditions here in a minute. What are you hanging around for?

LARRY

Oh, Mac. I fixed it with Sidney. He can lower the number 9 pipe and I'll work downstage here.

MAC

Fine . . . Fine.
(*He looks at* LARRY, *studying him.*)

LARRY

(*Uneasy under* MAC's *gaze*)
Didn't I tell you I was going to try Jeanie out? I think maybe she'd be a good cover for Lilly's understudy. Don't you?

MAC

Larry, step over here for a minute, will you? (*He leads him over to left proscenium, so that no one but* LARRY *will hear what he has to say*) There's one rule I never broke in my life. And it'd be a good idea if no stage manager ever broke it.

LARRY

What's that?

MAC

(*Speaking slowly*)
Don't ever let yourself get stuck on anybody that works in the same company as you do.

LARRY

I'm not stuck on anybody in this company.

MAC

Well, good. I'm glad to hear it. Because there's nothing worse for busting a troupe wide open.

LARRY

(*A little impatiently*)
Well, I told you, I'm not . . .

MAC

If it ever happened to me, I'd fire the girl—or quit the show myself. I wouldn't compromise one inch!

LARRY

O.K. O.K. I get it.

MAC

There are plenty of cute kids in the other shows around town. (*Trying to take the edge off now, and lighten the whole*

45

scene. He leans over and taps LARRY *on the arm*) As a matter of fact, I'm working on some new talent myself right now. You know little Betty Loraine.

LARRY

Betty Loraine—with the show across the street?

MAC

That's the one. Funny little thing. Never seems to wear anything but dungarees and sweaters, things like that. I'm just beginning to spar with her. Last night . . .

RUBY

(*Calling across stage*)
Hey, Mac! Here's Mr. Harrison! (*Waving out toward back of theatre*) How *are* you, Mr. Harrison? Enjoy your vacation?

HARRISON'S VOICE

(*From out front*)
Not much. I'm glad to be home. Are you ready for me, Mac?

MAC

Right away, Mr. Harrison. Got two replacement candidates here. They're getting into their practice clothes. (*Turning*) See if they're ready, Larry.

(LARRY *exits.*)

ME AND JULIET

MISS DAVENPORT'S VOICE
(*From out front*)
Hello, Mac.

MAC
(*Peering out into the darkness*)
Who's that?

HARRISON'S VOICE
I've got Miss Davenport with me.

MAC
Swell! Good to see you, Miss Davenport.

HARRISON'S VOICE
She's really here to protect her choreography. Afraid you and I might take a girl with a wooden leg.
(MAC *does his best to laugh convincingly at his boss's joke.*)

MAC
The first girl I'm going to show you was with Ballet Theatre.

DAVENPORT'S VOICE
What's her name?

MAC
Hilda Morton.

DAVENPORT'S VOICE

Oh, I know her. (*Lowering her voice*) She's a very good dancer, Ben. (HILDA *enters*) There she is, coming on now.

HARRISON'S VOICE

(*Also in low tones*)

She's not a Carmen type.

MAC

(*Leading* HILDA *forward*)

Mr. Harrison, this is Miss Morton.

HARRISON'S VOICE

How do you do?

HILDA

(*Peering out into the dark auditorium*)

I'm awfully glad to know you, Mr. Harrison. Hello, Miss Davenport.

DAVENPORT'S VOICE

Hello, Hilda. Start with some tour jeté's. (HILDA *obeys*) Fine. Now a grand jeté.

(HILDA *obliges expertly.*)

HARRISON'S VOICE

(*In a dry and final voice*)

Thank you very much, Miss Morton.

(HILDA, *knowing that is her dismissal, bows and smiles mechanically and starts off stage.*)

DAVENPORT'S VOICE

Wait a minute. Just a moment, Hilda. (HILDA *lingers. There are sounds of mumbled conversation*) I know she can dance the part.

HARRISON'S VOICE

She can't look it.

DAVENPORT'S VOICE

(*Weary and resigned*)

All right. Thank you very much, Hilda.
(HILDA *exits and* LARRY *immediately brings forth another girl and* MAC *introduces her.*)

MAC

This is Marcia Laval, Mr. Harrison, Miss Davenport.

HARRISON'S VOICE

Hello, Marcia. How've you been?

MARCIA

(*Delighted to be recognized by the manager*)

Just fine. How are you, Mr. Harrison? I didn't think you'd remember me.

HARRISON'S VOICE

Of course I remember you.

49

DAVENPORT'S VOICE
(*Sounding skeptical*)
Can you do a tour jeté?
(MARCIA *tries and is apparently much more of a show
girl than a dancer.*)

MARCIA
Would you like to see my elevation?

DAVENPORT'S VOICE
No. That will do. Thank you very much.

HARRISON'S VOICE
Wait a minute! (*Then again there is mumbled conversation*) I like this girl.

DAVENPORT'S VOICE
I don't!

HARRISON'S VOICE
(*To* MARCIA)
All right. Leave your name with the office so we know
where to get in touch with you.

MARCIA
Oh, thank you, Mr. Harrison.
(*She goes.*)

HARRISON'S VOICE

That all you got, Mac?

MAC

That's all this morning. There's a girl coming in next week
from the St. Louis Municipal Opera. They say that she . . .
(*He breaks off because he is conscious of* CHARLIE,
*who has just peeked in from the wings and is waving
to* HARRISON.)

CHARLIE

That Ben Harrison out there?

HARRISON'S VOICE

Hello, Charlie.

CHARLIE

(*Coming out on to the stage*)
Have you found a new Carmen for me?

HARRISON'S VOICE

No, we haven't.

CHARLIE

Well, I have a young lady with me who I think would be
just . . . (*Turning toward wings*) Come out here, darling.
. . . (BETTY *enters. She is as* MAC *has described her,* "A funny
little thing" *in dungarees and sweatshirt.* CHARLIE *takes her
by the hand.*) She's in the show across the street. Miss Betty
Loraine . . . Mr. Harrison, Miss Davenport.

51

BETTY

(*Beaming at them confidently*)
How do you do? (*To* MAC) Hello, Charm Boat!

MAC

(*Very formally*)
How do you do, Miss Loraine?
(*He turns away.* LARRY *is amused at* MAC's *predicament.*)

HARRISON'S VOICE

I'd like to see what you can do. How long would it take
you to get into your practice clothes?

BETTY

I *am* in my practice clothes.
(*She takes off her dungarees, under which she wears
dancer's tights.*)

CHARLIE

Before she dances, would you like to hear her read lines?
I got her up in one of the scenes.

HARRISON'S VOICE

Fine! Go ahead. Say, Mac! It looks as if Charlie's trying
to take your job away. Trying to muscle in on you.

MAC

It does look like he's trying to muscle in, doesn't it?

ME AND JULIET

BETTY
(*Going over to* MAC)
Can I have a script, Mac?

MAC
Certainly, Miss Loraine.
(*He hands it to her.*)

CHARLIE
All right, honey. I'm sitting on a park bench, and you come up to me.

BETTY (*As* CARMEN)
(*Reading from script*)
"Why do you pretend not to know I'm alive? (CHARLIE *as* ME *looks around at her*) All men know I'm alive. They can't help it, because I *am* alive!"
(*She heaves several deep breaths under her jersey to prove it.*)

HARRISON'S VOICE
Fine, fine!

BETTY (*As* CARMEN)
"Why do you sit by yourself in the park reading poetry? Don't you like girls?"

CHARLIE (*As* ME)
"Only one—Juliet—and she's an angel—she's too good for me."

BETTY (*As* CARMEN)

"Why don't you see how it feels to be with someone who's not too good for you?"

(CHARLIE *lowers his eyes to his imaginary book of poetry.*)

CHARLIE (*As* ME)

(*Looking at her*)

"You mean—?" (BETTY *nods her head vigorously*) "Oh no. I couldn't!"

BETTY (*As* CARMEN)

"If I thought you couldn't I wouldn't suggest it." (*Putting her head on his shoulder. Then, stepping out of character abruptly, calling out to* HARRISON) Do you want the number?

HARRISON'S VOICE

Sure!

(CHARLIE *nods to* CHRIS *who starts to play the piano.*)

CHARLIE

Buzz! You're just in time! (*Calling to* BUZZ *who is just crossing the stage, carrying a guitar case.*)

BUZZ

In time for what?

CHARLIE

Would you do the "Keep It Gay" routine with this young lady? Like a good fellow?

BUZZ

I got a T.V. audition at three o'clock . . .

HARRISON'S VOICE

You've got time, Buzz. Go ahead.

BUZZ

Who's that?

CHARLIE

That's Mr. Harrison.

BUZZ

(*A different man*)
Oh, hello, Mr. Harrison. Sure I've got time. Love to—sure!

CHARLIE

Oh by the way, have you two kids met—Betty Loraine this
is Buzz Miller. She knows the routine, Buzz. O.K., Chris.
(CHRIS *starts playing.* BETTY *sings and dances two re-
frains of "Keep It Gay" with* BUZZ.)

DAVENPORT'S VOICE

(*After dance*)
That was fine!

HARRISON'S VOICE

Your show is closing next week, isn't it? (*She nods*) Send
your agent around to see Ruby. Get that, Ruby?

RUBY

Check!

HARRISON'S VOICE
(*To* BETTY)

Could you start rehearsing tomorrow?

BETTY

Why not?

HARRISON

Get that, Mac?

MAC
(*Coldly*)

I understand.

HARRISON'S VOICE

Coming over to Sardi's, Charlie?

CHARLIE

Be right with you! (*As he passes* BETTY *on his way off*) Congratulations!

BETTY

Charlie, you've been wonderful. Thank you!
(*She gives him a big smacking kiss.* MAC *stamps off the stage.* CHARLIE *exits.* BETTY *puts on her dungarees.* SIDNEY *comes out to the center and calls up to the flies.*)

SIDNEY

Hey, Joe! Let down that number 9 pipe, will you?

56

BETTY

Hey, Ruby, where did Mac go? (RUBY *shrugs his shoulders and smiles*) I don't get it. Last night he was full of sweet talk. Today he acted as if he never met me before.

RUBY

Last night you were a girl in another show. Don't you know about his rule? With any girl in his own company—nothing!

BETTY

Oh, so that's it.

RUBY

You can take this job, or keep Mac . . . Which?
(*Pause.*)

BETTY

I'm going to take the job! And make him break his rule!

RUBY

You'll be the first girl to turn the trick. "Is he man or machine?" That's what they say about him.

BETTY

If he's a machine I don't want him. If he's a man, I'm going to make him prove it!
(*She exits. Meanwhile the number 9 pipe has been let down from the flies.* SIDNEY *has brought out a pile of color frames and during the ensuing scene proceeds to*

57

ME AND JULIET

change them in the lamps on the pipe. JEANIE *has come on the stage and she and* LARRY *walk over to the stage manager's table,* RUBY *waves a greeting to them as he exits.*)

LARRY

Just leave our things right there. (JEANIE *takes off her hat and places her bag on the table*) Did you get a chance to look over the part?

JEANIE

(*A little guiltily*)
Well, no, Larry. I didn't. I . . .

LARRY

That's all right. You know all the music, anyway, don't you? Let's start out with one of the songs. (*Calling across stage*) Chris, can you help us out?

CHRIS

What do you want?

LARRY

"No Other Love."
(*To* JEANIE)
Stand over near the piano, Jeanie.
(JEANIE *looks uncertain.*)

JEANIE

All right. Anything you want to tell me?

58

ME AND JULIET

LARRY

No. Just go ahead and sing it in your own way.

(JEANIE *crosses to the piano.* LARRY *carries a chair to the center of the stage, straddles it and leans on the back of it, then nods to* CHRIS. JEANIE *starts to sing. She sings well enough as far as voice is concerned, but her feeling for the lyric is superficial and her gestures are meaningless.*)

JEANIE

(*Singing*)

No other love have I,
Only my love for you,
Only—

LARRY

Just a minute, Jeanie! (*She stops singing*) Chris! (*He waves his hand and* CHRIS *stops*) Take five! (CHRIS *exits. There is a pause.* LARRY *looks at* JEANIE *as if trying to think of the right words to say. Then he speaks to her quietly*) Why did you do that just now . . . with your hands . . . like this?

(*He imitates her gesture.*)

JEANIE

I don't know. No reason in particular. I just didn't want to stand like a stick and do nothing.

(*Pause.*)

LARRY

Suppose you had to describe Juliet—what kind of girl would you say she was?

59

JEANIE

I'd say she was a nice, ordinary kid.

LARRY

Do you think Carmen is a stronger character?

JEANIE

Oh, yes . . . Don't you?

LARRY

Jeanie—the whole secret of singing this song is to realize that Juliet is a stronger, deeper, more passionate woman than Carmen.

JEANIE

More passionate?

LARRY

You've seen this happen, Jeanie—two nice, ordinary kids like Juliet and this little guy decide they want to live with each other for the rest of their lives. And suddenly something happens to them—two midgets are given the strength of giants. They'll knock over anybody who stands in their way.

JEANIE

(*Thoughtfully*)

Yes, I *have* seen that happen.

ME AND JULIET

LARRY

So has everyone in the audience. And if you're a real kid like Juliet, they'll recognize you—if you're phony, they'll reject you.

JEANIE

An audience would scare me.

LARRY

Every good actress is scared—scared they won't like her. Her job is to make them like her. And the way to do that is to be honest with them. They're the smartest people in the theatre, and the toughest . . . and the nicest. (*He sings:*)

The water in a river is changed every day
As it flows from the hills to the sea.
But to people on the shore the river is the same,
Or, at least it appears to be.
The audience in a theatre is changed every night,
As a show runs along on its way.
But to people on the stage the audience looks the same,
Every night, every matinée—
    A big black giant
    Who looks and listens
    With thousands of eyes and ears,
    A big black mass
    Of love and pity
    And troubles and hopes and fears;
    And every night

The mixture's different,
Although it may look the same.
To feel his way
With every mixture
Is part of the actor's game.

    One night it's a laughing giant,
    Another night a weeping giant.
    One night it's a coughing giant,
    Another night a sleeping giant.
    Every night you fight the giant
    And maybe, if you win,
    You send him out a nicer giant
    Than he was when he came in . . .

But if he doesn't like you, then all you can do
Is to pack up your make-up and go.
For an actor in a flop there isn't any choice
But to look for another show.

    That big black giant
    Who looks and listens
    With thousands of eyes and ears,
    That big black mass
    Of love and pity
    And troubles and hopes and fears,
    Will sit out there
    And rule your life
    For all your living years,

    (LARRY *turns back to her, a little self-conscious after
    his long "speech."*)

Now-er-would you like to try the song again? Just remember
to be real and . . . why are you looking at me like that?

JEANIE
(Flustered) .

Was I? Oh, excuse me.

LARRY

What's the matter?

JEANIE

Nothing, Larry. I was just thinking—how you can be in the same company with somebody for so long and not really know them at all.

LARRY
(Finding no answer)

Shall we try the song now? *(Calling to* CHRIS*)* Chris! *(Turning back to* JEANIE*)* Now, just think of the girl—out on the balcony, lonely—wishing that the guy would come back. *(He sits again and waits for her to begin.)*

JEANIE
(Singing)

No other love have I,
   Only my love for you,
   Only the dream we knew—
No other love.
Watching the night go by,
   Wishing that you could be
   Watching the night with me,
Into the night I cry:
     Hurry home, come home to me!
     Set me free,

Free from doubt
And free from longing.
Into your arms I'll fly.
Locked in your arms I'll stay,
Waiting to hear you say:
No other love have I,
No other love!

(LARRY *rises and goes over to* JEANIE.)

LARRY

Good. Now try starting it softer. Then let it build . . . (*To*
CHRIS) Take it half a tone higher.

(*He starts singing, to illustrate*)
No other love have I,
Only my love for you,
Only the dream we knew—
No other love.

(JEANIE *has started to sing with him*)
Watching the night go by
Wishing that you could be
Watching the night with me,
Into the night I cry:
Hurry home, come home to me!
Set me free,
Free from doubt
And free from longing.
Into your arms I'll fly.
Locked in your arms I'll stay,
Waiting to hear you say:
No other love have I,

64

No other love!

(*At the end of the song* JEANIE *turns and looks at*
LARRY, *catching his eyes gazing adoringly at her. Ob-*
viously he has been singing his half of a love duet.
Quickly he turns and crosses to CHRIS *at the piano and*
whispers instructions. CHRIS *starts to play the refrain*
again. JEANIE *picks it up on the third line.*)

JEANIE

. . . Only the dream we knew—
No other love.

(BOB, *entering up right, watches* JEANIE *singing and*
LARRY *conducting. He walks downstage and mocks*
JEANIE'S *manner of singing, making his gestures very*
broad. JEANIE *sees him but continues to sing, trying*
to brazen it through and not let BOB *think he can dis-*
turb her.)

Watching the night go by
Wishing that you could be
Watching the night with me,
Into the night I cry:
Hurry home, come home—
(JEANIE *stops suddenly and bursts out angrily*)
What's the matter with you? Making a big joke?

BOB

(*Applauding*)

Encore! Encore!

JEANIE

I don't see anybody laughing.

BOB

(His feelings hurt because his clumsy schoolboy comedy was not admired)

Excuse me for living. *(Turning back)* I didn't know you were a prima donna from the "Met." I just thought you were one of the girls in the chorus. *(Going upstage to* SIDNEY*)* Want some help, Sid?

SIDNEY

Help me clear these color frames.

JEANIE

Do you mind if we stop, Larry? *(Picking up her hat and bag from a chair)* I'm sorry to be like this. I guess if I was a real actress I wouldn't let anybody—make any difference.

LARRY

Come down tomorrow and we'll have another shot at it. (JEANIE *starts off*) You can go now, Chris.

CHRIS

Okay.

LARRY

Two o'clock call tomorrow.
    (CHRIS *exits.*)

JEANIE

Thank you, Larry. Thank you very much.
    (She goes out.)

66

SIDNEY

(*Calling to flyman*)

Take it away!

LARRY

(*Calling off*)

Will you kill this work light?

VOICE OFFSTAGE

Okay.

(*For some seconds* LARRY *remains rooted to a spot in the center of the stage. The light is switched off. The stage becomes quite dark, except for some shafts of daylight coming from the roof at the back.* LARRY *starts pacing up and down in the dark. Then another figure comes out of the shadows and stands in front of him.*)

BOB

Sidney tells me you had quite a rehearsal here.

LARRY

What do you mean?

BOB

You and Jeanie.

LARRY

Yes, it was fine. I think she'll—she may turn out fine.

(*He starts to go, but* BOB *reaches forward and grabs him by the arm.*)

67

ME AND JULIET

BOB

Wait a minute—Don't go yet.

LARRY

Let go of me!

BOB

(*Holding on to his arm*)
What's your hurry? I want to say something to you. (*He pulls* LARRY *toward him*) Stand still here a minute and listen to me. Are you making a play for my girl?

LARRY

Of course not! (BOB *continues to hold him*) Let go of me! (LARRY *tries to break* BOB's *hold on him*) What the hell's the matter with you? (*There is a stretch of silence*) I'm a stage manager rehearsing an understudy. What the hell's . . .

BOB

Just keep it that way, see? Stage manager and understudy. Strictly business. (*His voice becoming even quieter but more threatening*) If you ever try to move in on me with that kid, I—I'm just telling you . . . Something would happen to me . . . I couldn't *help* killing you—(*He throws* LARRY *away from him*) not if I tried. . . .

> (*He goes out.* LARRY *stands perfectly still in the darkness, then he resumes his pacing. The lights go out.*)

68

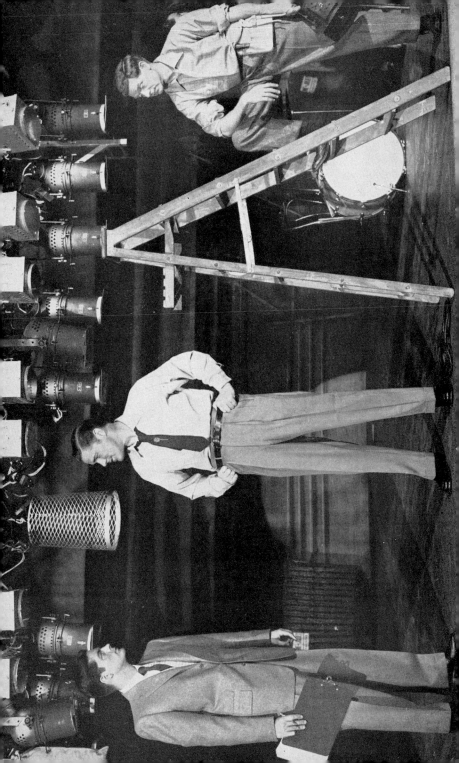

Scene VI

The alley leading to the stage door.

Various members of the company are draped around the set on benches, on a large garbage box, in the doorway leading to the theatre which is on the right, and the doorway leading to the covered part of the alley, which in turn leads to the street. Three dancers are improvising steps as the curtain rises. During the dance CHARLIE *enters and crosses to the stage door, stopping there a while to watch the dancers. At the finish of the dance there are shouts of approval and applause.*

A GIRL

They ought to have a spot in the show.

CHARLIE

It's easy to perform in an alley. But the only thing that pays off is what you do out there on the stage in front of an audience!

(He exits into the theatre.)

A BOY

Lovable Charlie Clay!

(Now JIM *comes staggering on, pale, his voice quavering.)*

69

JIM

Hello, everybody.

BOY

Hi, Jim.

GIRL

How's Susie?

JIM

She's started!

ANOTHER BOY

The baby?

JIM

She just took me to the hospital. I mean—I wanted to stay
but she said I had to come and give the show.
(*He exits into theatre.*)

ANOTHER BOY

He's white as a sheet—
(*He follows* JIM *off.*)

GIRL

It seems only yesterday when Susie left the show.

A GIRL

I wish I had a baby!

A BOY

You do?

70

A GIRL
(*Looking at him coldly*)
I mean legitimate.

A BOY
Oh.

HERBIE
(*To* LILY *as she enters*)
Hi, Lily! How'd you make out?

LILY
I think he liked me.

RUBY
Who?

HERBIE
She auditioned for Bing today.

GIRL
(*In incredible awe*)
Crosby?

LILY
(*Disdainfully*)
No. Rudolph.
(*She exits.*)

GIRL
Bing Rudolph? Who's he?
(JEANIE'S *voice is now heard off stage, singing happily.
All heads turn up toward the entrance.*)

71

JEANIE

(Off stage)

Out of nowhere
Came the feeling,
Knew the feel—
> *(She enters, starts to cross, is conscious of everyone
> looking at her, and stops)*

Hi, kids!

ALL

Hi, Jeanie!
> *(She resumes her happy singing as she exits.)*

JEANIE

Marriage type love!
> *(Before* JEANIE *has gone off* LORAINE *has made her
> entrance on the left. She now comes down eagerly to
> spill some news.)*

LORAINE

I just saw them together!

GIRL

Jeanie and Larry?

LORAINE

They were in the chili joint on Eighth Avenue. As soon as
they left the place they separated and walked on different
sides of the street.
> *(Now* LARRY's *voice is heard off stage whistling "No*

Other Love." Everyone quiets down and looks inno-
cent as he enters.)

RUBY

Hi ya, Larry?

LARRY

(*As if awakening suddenly*)
Oh . . . Hi, Ruby. (*Looking around*) Hello, everybody.
(*They return his greeting.* LARRY *turns, resumes whis-*
tling "No Other Love" and exits.)

HERBIE

It couldn't happen to two nicer people.

GIRL

Yeah! But what's going to happen when Bob finds out?

HERBIE

Gosh! I don't want to be around!
(*He exits.*)

ANOTHER GIRL

How is she handling him?

ANOTHER GIRL

She's telling him her mother's here from Chicago. That's
why she can't see him.

73

BOY

She can't keep that up forever.
> (*The crowd starts to disperse now and go in the theatre to get dressed.* BETTY *enters.*)

RUBY

Hi, Betty.

BETTY

Hi, Ruby.
> (*She looks behind her as if at someone who has been following her. Then she glides over to the bench and sits down, looking as unexpectant as she possibly can. The subject of her expectation now enters*—MAC. *Everyone has gone inside and they are alone.* MAC *starts to cross toward the stage door.*)

Hello, Mac.

MAC

How do you do, Miss Loraine.
> (*He proceeds on his way.*)

BETTY

Hot for October.
> (*He stops.*)

MAC

Yeh, but good weather for the World Series.

BETTY

Yeh. What are you doing with yourself these days?

74

MAC

Nothing much.

BETTY

Any truth about what I see in the columns—about you and Molly Burt being an item?

MAC

Could be.

BETTY

I used to know Molly quite well. We were in *Brigadoon* together.

MAC

That so?

BETTY

Yeh . . . Boy! Is she a dull dish!

MAC

Best I can do.

BETTY

(*Close to him*)

That's what *you* think.

(*He looks down at her. Their eyes meet for a long moment. Then he recovers.*)

MAC

You better go in and get dressed. (*She turns and starts off. He calls her back, rather morosely*) Betty! (*She turns, hesi-*

75

tates, then comes toward him smiling) I've been meaning to speak to you about that seduction scene.

BETTY

What's wrong with it?

MAC

It's gone to hell, that's what.

BETTY

Charlie and I think that's our best spot.

MAC

I don't wonder. You sure look as if you enjoy it.

BETTY

(*Loving this*)

Charlie says the way we play it now is the way the author and director wanted it, and when you put me in the show you tamed it down.

MAC

That so?

BETTY

Uh huh! So we've been heating it up a little each performance.

MAC

Well, start cooling it off, y'hear? It's getting so obvious it's lost all its charm. It's just plain disgusting and vulgar!

BETTY

(*Delighted*)

Y'think so? Well, for instance . . . I mean where does it get bad? Shall we run through it, and you can show me.

(BETTY *takes a* CARMEN *pose center and starts to clap her hands in rhythm.* MAC *looking pompous reluctantly starts to clap his hands to the same rhythm.* BETTY *dances very close to him. He backs away.*)

MAC

Now wait a minute—wait a minute.

BETTY

Oh, that's not the step, huh? Maybe you mean the Tango . . .

(BETTY *takes* MAC *and goes into another section of the dance, at the finish of this,* BETTY *is in a seductive pose, looking up at* MAC)

Is that all right?

(*He nods. They continue to dance until she puts her hand under his coat, caressing him.*)

MAC

That's what I mean!

(*He pushes her away.*)

BETTY

Oh, I see! What about this place?

(*She grabs* MAC *and they go into a whirling dance in*

*the center of the stage. She leans back on his arm. He
bends over her)*

Is that too much—?

(It might be, but MAC *is liking it. At this moment*
RUBY *comes in and stands for a moment, inspecting
them.)*

RUBY

What're you doing?

*(*MAC *and* BETTY *break quickly.)*

MAC

Rehearsing.

RUBY

Who's rehearsing who?

MAC

I'm trying to fix that seduction scene. They're playing it
like a burlesque show.

RUBY

I kinda like the way they do it.

MAC

(To BETTY*)*

You better go in and get dressed.

BETTY

Do you think we fixed it?

MAC

There's no fixing to do. You know damn well what I want.
Tame it down! That's what I want you to do. Tame it down!

BETTY

O.K., Mac. O.K., I'll do my best, Mac.
(*She turns and goes off, looking very happy.*)

MAC

(*To* RUBY)
Wanta slip across the street for a drink?

RUBY

I thought you never took a drink before a show.

MAC

I never do, but I just happen to feel like one.

RUBY

Look out, Mac. You start to break one rule, you may break
another.

MAC

Nuts to you.
(*He exits.* RUBY, *looking after* MAC, *smiles contemplatively.* HERBIE *enters.*)

79

RUBY

Are theatre people crazier than other people?

HERBIE

Sure!

RUBY

I don't think so. They just *show* it more than other people.
I think it comes from getting keyed up every night—getting
scared and excited.

HERBIE

On account of that big black giant Larry's always talking
about.

RUBY

(RUBY *smiles and starts to sing*)
One night it's a laughing giant,
Another night a weeping giant.
One night it's a coughing giant,
Another night a sleeping giant.
Every night you fight the giant
And maybe, if you win,
You send him out a nicer giant
Than he was when he came in . . .

But if he doesn't like you, then all you can do
Is to pack up your make-up and go.
For an actor in a flop there isn't any choice
But to look for another show.

80

ME AND JULIET

That big black giant
Who looks and listens
With thousands of eyes and ears—
He claps his hands and luck is with you,
He frowns and it disappears.
He'll chill your heart
And warm your heart
For all your living years.
    (*The curtains have closed on the set during the song.*
    The lights fade on RUBY.)

Scene VII

Betty's dressing room.
JEANIE, pressing one of BETTY's costumes, looks up as she comes in, singing gaily.

JEANIE

What are you so happy about?

BETTY

Mac says I'm overdoing the seduction scene. He says it's obvious and vulgar—don't you get it? We're making headway, kid. (*She crosses, sits at dressing table and stretches out her legs so that JEANIE can pull off her dungarees*) Gosh, am I lucky, having you! . . . When you asked me for the job I thought you were kidding. A college graduate, no less!

JEANIE

(*As she hangs up BETTY's dungarees and jacket*)
I wanted the dough. My understudy pay stops this week. Summer's over. They don't need two understudies any more.

BETTY

You're a wonderful kid.

82

JEANIE

Wonderful, nothing. It's a break for me to be able to share this room with you—instead of dressing in that madhouse downstairs.

BETTY

(*Proceeding to make up her face*)
Whee! When those dames get together and start cackling, that's something. And it's always on the same subject.

JEANIE

Yeh! Same thing you and I always cackle about.

BETTY

Yeh. I wonder why. I wonder why we let men take up so much of our lives. Why is it so important to me to make Mac jealous of Charlie? What am I after, anyway? To make him come up to me some night and ask me to go out with him? Would that be such a wonderful thing to happen? . . . Yeh, it would. . . . I haven't heard much out of you lately about *your* love life. What's the matter with it?

JEANIE

Oh, it's all right.

MAC'S VOICE

(*In a loud-speaker that is on the wall above* BETTY's *dressing table*)
Five minutes to overture! Five minutes to overture!

83

BETTY

(Powdering her arms and shoulders, vigorously)
O.K., Mr. Mac. I'll be ready. Stick around for the seduction scene tonight. I'm going to do a dance with Charlie that'll make you wish you were never born!

JEANIE

I fixed that zipper in your dress.

BETTY

Thanks. Boy, do I love to get into that dress. What a part! What a girl that Carmen! You know what I mean? All woman, and no complications. Just a bundle of uncomplicated passion.

JEANIE

Did it ever occur to you that Juliet might have more real passion than Carmen?

BETTY

No. Did it ever occur to you?

JEANIE

It's Larry's idea. You know he's a wonderful director, Betty. All the understudies say the same thing. They say that he'll be one of the tops some day.

BETTY

Do you know how many times you've told me that?

84

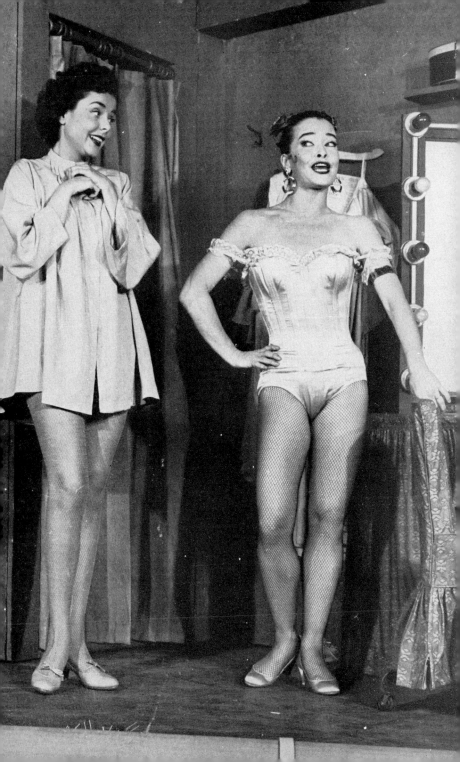

JEANIE

(*Defensively*)

Told you what?

BETTY

(*Eyeing her closely*)

I bet you're going to miss those understudy rehearsals especially with such a sympathetic director.

(JEANIE *puts a Spanish comb in* BETTY's *hair with punishing emphasis.*)

Ouch!

JEANIE

Hold your head still!

BETTY

You'll be getting stagestruck like me, maybe. .

JEANIE

Could be.

BETTY

Boy, do I love to act! (*She rises and looks in the mirror*) All day long you can flop at everything you do. But at night— at night you know you're going to fool fifteen hundred people into thinking you're wonderful!

(*She sings*)

I'm colorless and shy,
Inhibited and dull.
My entrance into any room is followed by a lull.
This droopiness in me

Miraculously melts
When I step on a stage and make believe I'm someone else.
Quite suddenly I'm mentally and physically equipped
With most unusual qualities—it says so in the script!

JEANIE

Who is that delectable dame,
Cool as cream and hotter than flame?
Who? Who could it be?

BETTY

It's me! It's me! It's me!

JEANIE

Who's that queenly gift to the boys—

BETTY

Always keen and lousy with poise?

JEANIE

Who? Who could it be?

BETTY

It's me! It's me! It's me!
When the authors make me say
Words that make me wittier,
I feel just as smart as they
(And what's more, I'm prettier!)

ME AND JULIET

Who's that girl who's getting the wows?
Who's that babe who's taking the bows?

BETTY

In a daze, I wonder who is she!
Imagine my surprise
When once I realize
It's nobody else but wonderful, beautiful me!

My picture hangs in Sardi's
For all the world to see.
I sit beneath my picture there
And no one looks at me.
I sometimes wear dark glasses,
Concealing who I am,
Then all at once I take them off—
And no one gives a damn!
But when I start to play a part, I play the part okay;
No longer am I no one when I'm someone in a play.

JEANIE

Every man is flipping his lid
Over that phenomenal kid—
Who? Who could it be?

BETTY

It's me! It's me! It's me!

JEANIE

Whose hot kiss from passionate lips
Perpetrates a total eclipse?
Who? Who could it be?

BETTY

It's me! It's me! It's me!
Oh, what I can perpetrate
By my osculation!
Just one little kiss, and pouf!
There goes perpetration!

JEANIE

Who has learned the formula which
Satisfies the seven year itch?
Who's that dazzling personali*tee?*

JEANIE AND BETTY

Well, here's the big surprise:
Hot dog, and damn my eyes!
It's nobody else but wonderful, beautiful me!
(BETTY *runs to the dressing table, picks up a fan and
runs off as* JEANIE *bows her out of the dressing-room
door with exaggerated homage.* JEANIE *then gets her
own dress off the hanger and puts a towel on her hair
so that it won't be mussed as she puts the dress over
her head. Then she hangs the towel up and starts to
hook up her dress as* LARRY *enters. They embrace. He
then takes over the job of hooking her dress.*)

JEANIE

Remember what you said that first day? "When two ordinary little people decide that they want to live with each other for the rest of their lives, they'll knock over anything that stands in their way."

LARRY

I remember . . . We've got to tell Bob, Jeanie.

JEANIE

I know. We've got to think of some good *way* to tell him. (*She clings tightly to* LARRY) I haven't found a good way to tell myself. I can't make myself believe that we did what we did today. Every once in a while I take the ring out of my bag and just look at it.

MAC'S VOICE
(*In loud-speaker*)
Everybody on stage. First act! Everybody on!

LARRY
(*Whispering*)
See you later.
(*They kiss again and he goes out quickly.* JEANIE *goes to her handbag and takes her wedding ring out and looks at it.*)

JEANIE
(*Singing*)
Imagine my surprise!
Imagine my surprise!
It's nobody else but wonderful beautiful—

Jeanie!

*(Suddenly realizing that she is late for her entrance
on stage, she shouts)*

Me!

*(She runs over to her dressing table, picks up the ac-
cessories to her costume and runs off.)*

Scene VIII

The Light Bridge.
BOB *and* SIDNEY, *getting their lamps set for the finale of
Act One.*

SIDNEY

Well, I'll be glad to get down off this perch and stretch
my legs.

BOB

You can't get down till they let you down. It's like being in
jail.

SIDNEY

You know this first-act finale coming up is my favorite
scene in the show? I'd like to go to a fancy night club like
that some time—be out on the town.

BOB

With a girl like Carmen, huh?

SIDNEY

She'd be okay.

BOB

Tell me something, Sidney. Have you ever had another girl—I mean since you've been married?

SIDNEY

Sure. Plenty.

BOB

I bet you haven't had one.

SIDNEY

All right then, I haven't had one. I don't see anything to be proud of anyway—cheating on your wife. Would you cheat if you got married?

BOB

Sure I would. That's why I don't get married. Right now I'm worse off than if I was married. I got a girl and I can't get to see her.

SIDNEY

(*Playing dumb*)

Yeh? Why not?

BOB

Her mother's in town. Got here from Chicago a month ago. She was only going to stay a week. But she's still here! Every week Jeanie says her mother is going next week . . . But she stays!

ME AND JULIET

That's a pretty tough deal. . . . Quick the effects!
(*They both throw their lamps on.*)

BOB

(*After they have met their cue*)
So you wouldn't cheat. What about your wife? Are you
sure about *her?*

SIDNEY

(*Suddenly very resentful at this suggestion*)
Aw, nuts to you. (*Getting worked up*) You just shut up
about my wife!

BOB

Let's see. You live in Bayside.

SIDNEY

Y'better shut up! Leave my wife out of this or you'll be
sorry!

BOB

What the hell will I be sorry about! . . . Let's see, Bayside,
that's about a half hour on the Long Island Railroad. That
means you leave your house every night about seven. You
can't get home before twelve—How do you know what she's
doing all that time?
(SIDNEY *can't hit* BOB. *He gropes for another way to get
revenge.*)

SIDNEY

I know what she's doing all right . . . I know what somebody else is doing too!

BOB

(*Immediately sensing something from Sidney's tone*)
Yeh?

SIDNEY

And it ain't with her mother.
(BOB *grabs* SIDNEY. *Music comes up from below.*)

BOB

You prove what you're saying or I'll tear you apart.

SIDNEY

If you feel like tearing somebody apart why not try it on the guy who's making a dope out of you?

BOB

Who?

SIDNEY

The Assistant Stage Manager.

BOB

Larry?

SIDNEY

Uh-huh.

BOB

Prove it.

SIDNEY

All right. I will. You come over and take my side of the bridge. I'll switch with you. And maybe if you look down there at his desk—at the right time—you'll see what I see every night—every single night.

BOB

What do you mean "the right time"?

SIDNEY

You know that part where Jeanie is carrying a lot of flowers on a tray? (BOB *nods*) And Don Juan takes all the flowers and gives 'em to Carmen? Then Jeanie goes off? That's when it happens. The same thing happens every night. . . . Every night.

BOB

(*Huskily*)

Come on. We'll switch sides.

> (*Slowly* BOB *and* SIDNEY *move toward each other.* BOB *holds on to the rail to steady himself.* SIDNEY's *face shows panic at the force he has set in motion and cannot stop. They switch sides. The music grows louder. The lights fade.*)

Scene IX

A night club.

LILY *as* JULIET *is seen in a pin spot singing "No Other Love." Then the curtains part on a stage crowded with dancers, among whom are* BETTY *as* CARMEN *and* CHARLIE *as* ME.

BETTY (CARMEN)

Having fun? (CHARLIE *nods his head*) Then why don't you look happier? (CHARLIE *grins uncomfortably*) What have you got your mind on?

CHARLIE (As ME)

Nothing.

BETTY (CARMEN)

Well, why don't you put it on me?
> (*The spot fades on* JULIET, *as if she were fading from* CHARLIE'S *guilty mind. He goes on dancing more happily with* BETTY. *Now* JIM, *as* DON JUAN, *comes on, dancing with* MISS OXFORD.)

CHARLIE (ME)

You see that fellow who just came in? That's my boss.

BETTY (CARMEN)

That so? Who's that with him?

ME AND JULIET

CHARLIE (ME)

Oh, I don't know. Some model or actress or somebody. He's always with a different one. They say he can get any girl he wants to get.

BETTY (CARMEN)

That so? He couldn't get me.

CHARLIE (ME)

How do you know?

BETTY (CARMEN)

'Cause *you* got me.

CHARLIE (ME)

You're a doll, Carmen. Here I am, just an ordinary clerk who works in his office, and you'd rather have me than him —him with all those millions and yachts . . .
(*They dance around for about four bars while* CAR-MEN *looks thoughtful.*)

BETTY (CARMEN)

How many millions has he got?

CHARLIE (ME)

Oh, I don't know, but it isn't less than fifty million.
(DON JUAN *engineers his partner over in front of* CAR-MEN *and* CHARLIE.)

97

JIM (DON JUAN)

Hello, my boy.

CHARLIE (ME)

(Nearly tongue-tied with fright at being suddenly addressed by the boss who has never noticed him before)
Hello, Mr.—Mr. . . .

JIM (DON JUAN)

Meet Miss Oxford.

CHARLIE (ME)

Pleased to meet you. This is Miss Carmen.

JIM (DON JUAN)

How do you do?
(He takes CARMEN in his arms and dances off with her, motioning to CHARLIE to take MISS OXFORD. During the ensuing dialogue JIM and BETTY and CHARLIE and MISS OXFORD continue to dance, as do the chorus, and meanwhile the stage moves over, revealing about ten feet of the off-stage scene. LARRY is at the stage manager's desk. About three-quarters of the full stage remains and the dancing in Me and Juliet *can be seen while the dialogue is read.)*
You and I ought to make a good combination.

BETTY (CARMEN)

Think so?

JIM (DON JUAN)

Don't you?

BETTY (CARMEN)

Maybe. Some day. I just don't like to start one course till I've finished with the other.

JIM (DON JUAN)

Well, just remember the meat and potatoes are ready. (*Looking over at* CHARLIE *dancing with* MISS OXFORD) As soon as you finish with the fish.

BETTY (CARMEN)

I'll remember.   79032

(*Now* JEANIE, *wearing the costume of a night-club flower girl, enters and walks among the dancers with a tray of flowers. Playing the scene* SIDNEY *has described to* BOB, *she goes up to* DON JUAN *and* CARMEN. DON JUAN *takes some orchids off her tray and gives them to* CARMEN. JEANIE *turns and moves toward the exit.* DON JUAN *delivers* CARMEN *back to* ME *and takes* MISS OXFORD. *The dance proceeds.*
Meanwhile JEANIE *exits, puts her tray of flowers on* LARRY'S *desk and then goes up to him as she apparently does every night, ready for her kiss. He takes her in his arms and kisses her.*
Suddenly a spotlight shines on them from the bridge. They both look up, panic in their eyes. They cling to each other like two terrified children and continue to stare up at the light as if fascinated and hypnotized

99

*by it. The music becomes very loud at this point. The
dancing on the stage becomes faster.* MAC *enters, takes
in the situation, and waves to* BOB *to take the lights off,
but the light stays on.* BETTY, *onstage, looks up at the
bridge, wondering why her spot has gone off. Then
she looks into the wings and understands, and looks
back at the bridge, frightened.*

Off stage, JEANIE *pulls away from* LARRY, *never taking her eyes from the bridge.* MAC, *in unheard dialogue, makes gestures to* LARRY *to beat it quick.* RUBY
*comes on with a worried expression, as if already told
about the crisis.* MAC *talks to him and* RUBY *takes*
LARRY'S *arm and leads him away.* LARRY *submits to this
like a man in a daze.* MAC *then puts the tray in* JEANIE'S
*hands and pushes her onto the stage. She walks across
the stage among the dancers, looking up frightened at
the bridge. The lamp keeps following her as if* BOB
*will not let her go. Terrified, she moves back toward
the entrance on the right where* MAC, *in the wings, is
waving wildly up to* BOB *to take the spot off her. As
she reaches a certain point a girl looks up and screams.
A sandbag comes down and knocks* JEANIE'S *tray out
of her hands.* MAC *pulls her off the stage, gets to his
desk and shouts signals into his microphone, apparently ordering the curtain to come down while the
dancers, terrified, go on with their routine, all keeping
their eyes turned up toward the bridge. The curtain
falls.)*

ACT TWO

ACT TWO

SCENE I

Downstairs lounge of the theatre.

About one minute before the end of Act One of Me and Juliet.

On stage right is the lower part of a curved staircase leading to the auditorium upstairs. On stage left, well downstage, is the candy and lemonade counter.

HERBIE *is busy setting cartons of lemonade on top of the counter, taking them out of a very large box. Also on top of the counter are displayed some peppermint candies, Life-Savers, lozenges, and the usual assortment of lobby confections. Two* USHERS *come down the stairs.*

FIRST USHER

Did you see the finale of the first act?

SECOND USHER

That was a funny one.

HERBIE

What was a funny one?

SECOND USHER

Just now in the finale one of the spotlights came off a principal and followed a chorus girl all around the stage!

FIRST USHER

And then something dropped from the top and nearly hit her.

HERBIE

(*Thoughtfully*)

That *is* funny.

FIRST USHER

This is a funny night all around. (*To* SECOND USHER) Tell Herbie what happened to *you*, Sadie.

SECOND USHER

Oh, yeh. I was showing a guy and his wife to their seats. They came in late. It was dark on the aisle. His wife was walking in front of us and he pinched me!

HERBIE

Where?

FIRST USHER

(*Indicating an area where a girl might be pinched by a vulgar gentleman*)

Right there.

SECOND USHER

(*Pointing to the other side of same area*)
No, here. I can feel it yet—nearly.

HERBIE

What did you do?

SECOND USHER

Before I could do anything the guy slips a five-dollar bill
into my hand.

HERBIE

Then what'd you do?

SECOND USHER

Gave him the two programs and beat it up the aisle.

HERBIE

Well, you got to hand it to a feller who pays as he goes.
(*The girls exit.* RUBY *and* LARRY *come down the stairs.*
RUBY *leads him straight over to the door, center, opens
it with a key and pushes* LARRY *in.*)

RUBY

Don't open the door if anybody knocks. Don't open the
door unless I unlock it.

OFFSTAGE VOICE

Smoking in the outer lobby only!

HERBIE

What's up?

RUBY

Bob caught Larry with Jeanie.

HERBIE

He'll kill him.

RUBY

He will if he finds him.

HERBIE

Did he see you leaving the stage for the front of the house?

RUBY

That's what I'm afraid of. I think he did. (*He starts for stairs and turns back*) If he comes down here, you don't know anything.

HERBIE

Check.

> (RUBY *scampers up stairs.* THEATRE PATRONS *pour down, and fill the lounge.*)

HERBIE

(*Singing*)

Lemonade,
Freshly made!
A bottle of ice cold Coke!

106

ME AND JULIET

BORED PATRON

I love to go to a theatre lounge
To enjoy a noisy smoke.

HERBIE

Lemonade,
Freshly made!

STARRY-EYED GIRL

I simply adore the show!

BORED PATRON

I wouldn't wait for the second act
If I had some place to go!

MUSIC LOVER

I like the one that goes
Da di da dum,
Da di da dum,
Da di da dum.
Marriage type love.

WIFE

(To her husband)

I don't think it's right
To be sulky all night
Over one little bill from Saks!

ME AND JULIET

BUSINESS MAN

(To another)

What do I care if they balance the budget,
As long as they cut my tax?

MUSIC LOVER

I like the one that goes:
No other love have I.
Hurry back home tonight!
It's me, it's me, it's me . . .

HER COMPANION

That doesn't sound quite right.

GIRL

The fellow beside me keeps dropping his program
And groping around my feet.

BORED PATRON

(Tapping her on the shoulder)

The couple behind me had garlic for dinner.
Would you like to trade your seat?

FASTIDIOUS PATRON

I think the production is fine,
The music is simply divine!
The story is lovely and gay—
But it just isn't my kind of play.

108

ME AND JULIET

They don't write music any more
Like the old Vienna valses!
The guy today who writes a score
Doesn't know what schmalz is!
The plots are all too serious,
No longer sweet and gay.
The authors who think
Certainly stink.
The theatre is fading away.
    (Their faces light up now)
Oh . . .
The theatre is dying,
The theatre is dying,
The theatre is practically dead!
Some one ev'ry day writes
We have no more playwrights,
The theatre is sick in the head.
Some singer of dirges
Gets earnest and urges
The public to have a good cry—

HERBIE

But the show still goes on—
The theatre's not gone.

HAPPY MOURNERS

We wish it would lie down and die,
Why in hell won't it lie down and die?

109

ME AND JULIET

STARRY-EYED GIRL

(*Answering them*)
I thought that I'd laugh myself silly
On the ev'ning I spent with Bea Lillie.

BUSINESS MAN

I sure had to hassle and hussle
Buying tickets for Rosalind Russell!

SATISFIED PATRON

I just had a picnic at *Picnic*
And loved everyone in the cast—

HAPPY MOURNERS

Your talk is absurd!
Why haven't you heard
The theatre's a thing o' the past?
Tra-la
The theatre's a thing o' the past!

ROMANTIC PATRON

My love for my husband grew thinner
The first time I looked at Yul Brynner,
And back in my bed on Long Island
I kept dreaming of Brynner in Thailand.

BUSINESS MAN

I love Shirley Booth and Tom Ewell.

110

ME AND JULIET

ENTHUSIASTIC PATRON

The Crucible—boy, what a play!

HAPPY MOURNERS

The poor little schmos!
Not one of them knows
The theatre is passing away—
Hey! Hey!
The theatre is passing away!
> (*Their faces lighting up again with necrophilian ex-
> altation*)
The theatre is dying,
The theatre is dying,
The theatre is practically dead!
The ones who are backing it
Take a shellacking,
And never get out of the red.

ALL THE REST

But actors keep acting,
And plays keep attracting
And seats are not easy to buy.
And year after year
There is something to cheer—

HAPPY MOURNERS

We'd much rather have a good cry—

111

ALL THE REST

Why in hell don't *you* lie down and die?

HAPPY MOURNERS

The theatre is . . .

ALL THE REST

Living!

HAPPY MOURNERS

The theatre is . . .

ALL THE REST

Living!
Why don't you lie down and die?
> (*At the end of the number the lights are flashed as a signal that the intermission is over.*)

OFFSTAGE VOICE

Curtain going up! Second act! Curtain going up!
> (*As the* CROWD *disperses and goes up the stairs, the* FIRST USHER *nudges the* SECOND USHER *and points at one of the* PATRONS.)

SECOND USHER

That's the one who pinched me!

FIRST USHER

To look at him you wouldn't think . . .
> (*But as she says this the gentleman has passed by and*

done it to her. She squeals. The TWO USHERS *exit as* DARIO *comes on and starts to gaze at several ladies, hoping that each one might be the one who is writing to him. As he gets near the counter,* HERBIE *addresses him.*)

HERBIE

Still looking for your gardenia woman?

DARIO

I am sick of this gardenia woman. Why does she hide from me? How long can a starving man live on flowers?

HERBIE

Must be some kind of a nut.

DARIO

Ah no, she is not a nut! You should see her letters. She is a poet! She has fallen in love with me, just watching me conduct. That's all she knows about me. Nothing more. Just how I look when I conduct the play, when I make beautiful music. (DARIO *sips drink*) Ah, no, she is not a nut.

HERBIE

She sounds like a nut.
(HERBIE *nudges him and points across to a lady who is wearing a gardenia.* DARIO *leaves* HERBIE *and he and the lady gravitate toward each other as if drawn by some mystic impulse.*)

LADY WITH GARDENIA

You're the orchestra leader, aren't you?

DARIO

Yes. Are you—?

LADY WITH GARDENIA

Let me have your cuff. (*He holds his arm up. She takes a lipstick from her purse and writes on his cuff*) This is my telephone number. When you go backstage will you give it to Charlie Clay, the one who plays "Me"?
(*She exits.*)

DARIO

Charlie Clay!
(*He exits, a frustrated and deeply exasperated man. JEANIE, passing him on the stairs, enters and runs to the door of the office. She wears a raincoat over her show costume.*)

HERBIE

He won't open it. Ruby told him not to. Ruby said . . .
(*They hear BOB shouting at someone, off stage.*)

JEANIE

He's coming! Hide me!

HERBIE

Here!
(*She gets behind the counter, just before BOB enters.*)

BOB

Either one of them come down here?

HERBIE

Either one of who?

BOB

(*Going over to him*)
You know damn well who.

HERBIE

No I don't, Bob.

BOB

No I guess you don't. They're out here somewhere.

HERBIE

Gee, Bob, the curtain's up, aren't you supposed to be . . .

BOB

Damn them! Damn them to hell!
(*He runs off right, as* RUBY *comes down the stairs. He stops short as he hears* BOB *off stage.*)

BOB

(*Off stage*)
Anybody in there?

HERBIE

Jeanie! Quick!

> (HERBIE *helps* JEANIE *into a large box behind the counter and puts lemonade cartons on top.*)

BOB

> (*Muttering as he re-enters*)

That damned Mac, that lousy stage manager! He wouldn't move that ladder over so I could get down from the bridge. Gave them time to get away—damn him!

> (BOB *looks about him from one side to the other. Then he starts to move toward the counter.*)

HERBIE

> (*Frightened*)

What do you want, Bob?

> (BOB *slings* HERBIE *aside as he goes by him and takes a look behind the counter. There is, of course, nothing there. Then his eyes light on the box. He goes to the box and starts sweeping the empty lemonade cartons off the top.* RUBY, *in a last desperate attempt to save the situation, comes running downstage and shouts at* BOB.)

RUBY

Hey, Bob! What's the matter with you, you big drip?

BOB

(*Looking up quickly, unused to having anybody talk to him like this*)

What!

RUBY

Get back there on that bridge!

BOB

Who're you talking to?

RUBY

I'm talking to you, you big gas bag . . . (BOB *takes a step toward* RUBY, *who, feeling his success, pours it on thicker so that he can really divert* BOB *from what he was going to do*) You got a job you're being paid for. You get the hell back to that bridge or I'll call up the union. I'll tell them . . .

> (BOB *reaches forward, pulls* RUBY's *coat up over his head, turns him around and lands him seated on the floor.*)

BOB

Tell that to the union! (*He goes to the stairs*) You know one good thing about this lousy theatre? The alley to the stage door and the front door are both on the same street. A feller can stand at the bar across the way and nobody can get out without him seeing it.

> (*He exits upstairs.*)

RUBY

(*To* HERBIE)

Keep an eye on him.

HERBIE

(*Crosses over to stairs.* RUBY *goes over to box behind the counter and helps* JEANIE *out*)

117

He's gone.

> (*A drunken girl enters from stairs.* RUBY *stands in front of* JEANIE *trying to keep her out of sight.*)

HERBIE

Hey, lady, you're going the wrong way. The second act has started.

DRUNKEN GIRL

> (*Crossing to Ladies Room*)

I'll come down here to the Ladies Room any time I feel like it—and I feel like it.

> (*She exits.* RUBY *leads* JEANIE *to the office door, unlocks it, and* JEANIE *goes in. As* RUBY *locks the door behind her, the scene fades.*)

Scene II

The bar across the street.
A bartender is pouring rye whiskey into a glass for BOB,
who is seated at the bar.

BOB

(*To the bartender as he starts to take the bottle away*)
Leave it here.

BARTENDER

We're not supposed to . . .

BOB

Listen! I've been pushed around enough tonight, see? (*The*
BARTENDER *puts the bottle back on the bar*) I'm not going to
take any more—from anybody. Get it?

BOB

(*Singing*)
When you lay off your liquor you get in a rut
And forget the fun you have missed for years.
Then it touches your lips—and you go off your nut,
Like a dame who hasn't been kissed for years!
        (*The* BARTENDER *goes off*)

119

You feel the world go drifting by,
As if you're on a boat,
And every time you drink some rye
(To keep the boat afloat)
A small, but red-hot butterfly
Flutters down your throat . . .
It feels good—
Not good like something sweet,
Not good like something beautiful,
But good like something strong.
It feels right—
Not right like right or left,
But right, like in an argument,
The other guy is wrong!
It feels good
To feel high,
High above a world of weasels and their lousy weasel talk.
A good drink, and you fly
Over all the things that frighten all the little jerks who
            walk.
You feel smart—
Not smart like smarty pants,
But smart like finding out the truth!
Like someone bangs a gong,
    And that gong is a signal that the road's all clear,
    With no one and nothing in the world to fear!
    The limit for you is the sky
    And you are a hell of a guy!
    And if you feel like breaking up a certain place,
    Or if you feel like pushing in a certain face,
    You are the bozo who can!

ME AND JULIET

You are a hell of a man!
Not a weasel,
Not a louse,
Not a chicken,
Not a mouse,
    But a man!

Scene III

A sequence in Act Two of Me and Juliet. *The* Me and Juliet *show curtain.*

JIM *as* DON JUAN *enters and waits for* BETTY *as* CARMEN, *who slinks on toward him.*

> JIM

Hi ya, Carmen.

> BETTY

Hi ya, Don.

> JIM

How ya feelin'?

> BETTY

Fit.

> JIM

Feel like dancin'?

> BETTY

Don, you're on.

> JIM

Baby, this is it!

> BETTY

Let's create some chaos.

122

ME AND JULIET

JIM

This could be the night.

BETTY

Let us be the first two wrongs that ever made a right.

We deserve each other,
We deserve each other,
I'll tell the world that we do.
You and your miniature sparrow brain
I and my tiny I.Q.
We deserve each other.
Let me tell you, brother,
I am a difficult girl.
You're an impossible character—
Why don't we give it a whirl?
I don't want to reform you,
To make your mistakes you are free,
But I just want to be certain
That your greatest mistake will be me!
If you want to wrestle
I'm the weaker vessel,
And I'll be easy to swerve.
We deserve each other,
So let us take what we deserve.

> *(The curtain rises behind them. The ensemble now
> join them in an elaborate dance.)*

Scene IV

Office of the company manager in the theatre.

LARRY *is pacing the stage. His coat is off. His fists are clenched as he walks. His face is tortured with worry and frustration.* JEANIE *sits on the couch and watches him.*

JEANIE

(*Making conversation to take* LARRY's *mind off his trouble*)
What are all those boxes over there on that safe?

LARRY

(*Stopping in his pacing as she hoped he would, he speaks in a dull, flat tone*)
Those? . . . Mail orders. One pile has the letters and the checks in them, and the other pile is a record of the letters that have been answered.

JEANIE

(*Making more conversation*)
I hear talk that the stage managers are going to ask you to put on their talent show this year. It would be good experience for you, wouldn't it? . . . Betty says I'm getting stage-struck, but she wants to be a great actress. I just want to be the wife of a great director.

124

LARRY

It takes a big man to be a director. You're married to a little man. A little man with no guts. That's why I'm in here hiding, hiding because I'm scared.

JEANIE

Larry, you're just making yourself miserable. You . . .
(*Pause. Then* LARRY *plunges into a confession to punish himself.*)

LARRY

The first day I rehearsed you—I never told you because I was ashamed . . . He grabbed me by the arms. I stood there, paralyzed with fright. He told me if I didn't keep away from you he'd kill me. I didn't answer him. I couldn't—couldn't talk. So damn scared of him I could hardly breathe!
(*He throws himself into a chair.*)

JEANIE

(*Smiling, studying him, her voice quiet*)
He said he'd kill you, and you married me anyway. (*She puts her hands on his shoulders*) I love you, Larry. I've loved you ever since that day we started to rehearse. I think you're a wonderful man, Larry—gentle and understanding, and fun to be with. That's a lot of man for a girl to be married to. I couldn't expect to get a prize fighter thrown in with all that.
(*Music has started beneath her speech. Now she sings:*)
Once and for always
Let me make it clear

What I am to you
And what you are to me.
I want to tell you while I have you near
This is how it is
And how it's going to be.

I'm your girl,
It's time you knew,
All I am
Belongs to you.
Any time you're out of luck
I'm unlucky too.
I'm your partner, your lover, your wife, your friend.
I'll be walking beside you till journey's end.
With your arms around me,
I'll be yours alone—
I'm the girl you own.

> (LARRY *joins her in a second refrain. They embrace.
> Then he leaves her and goes to the loud-speaker on
> the wall.*)

LARRY

Must be near the middle of the second act.

> (*He turns the loud-speaker on. Music is heard, com-
> ing through it.*)

JEANIE

Just about the middle.

> (*Now the lock in the door is turned.* RUBY *and* MAC
> *enter.*)

ME AND JULIET

RUBY

You talk to them, Mac. I'll keep watch outside.
(*He exits, closing and locking the door.*)

MAC

Listen, kids. I don't want either one of you to go home to-night.

LARRY

I'll have to face this guy some time, Mac.

MAC

Maybe some time, but not tonight. He's out of control. He nearly broke up the show just now.
(*The window up center is rattled.* MAC *switches off the light.* LARRY *and* JEANIE *stand like statues. There is silence, then a knock on the window, with a heavy object. A second's wait, then the window is broken.* BOB *puts his hand through, unlocks it, then pulls it open. The office being below the level of the alley, the window sill is even with the ground.* BOB *can therefore step through the window onto the sofa. He stands there for a moment silhouetted against the window.*)

BOB

I thought I heard voices in here—I couldn't tell what they were sayin' . . . (*Looking at* JEANIE) But I had a hunch that I knew one of the voices damn well. (*He steps off the couch and addresses* LARRY) I told you what would happen, didn't

127

I? I warned you! (*He advances on* LARRY. LARRY *backs up against the wall.*)

MAC

Just a minute there, Bob! You don't know what the hell you're doing.

(*He steps forward and grabs* BOB'S *arm.* BOB *turns and plants one on* MAC'S *jaw and* MAC *falls back on the floor. He's out cold.* BOB *goes back to* LARRY.)

BOB

I'm going to give you one chance. I'll let you go if you say to Jeanie what I tell you to say. Now listen close because it's your only chance. I want you to say: "Jeanie, I'm a lousy little coward and I don't love you enough to fight for you." Go on, say it! (LARRY *stares at* BOB, *his face tense with the torture he is going through.* JEANIE *watches him. He turns toward her.* BOB *senses that he's won. He goes to* JEANIE *and stands beside her*) Better be quick! It's your only chance. I'm not going to wait. Say it now! Say after me . . . (*He puts his arm around* JEANIE *and pulls her close to him*) "Jeanie, I'm a lousy little . . ."

(BOB'S *touching* JEANIE *awakens* LARRY *and changes him suddenly from a sensitive, imaginative man to an instinctive animal. He springs on* BOB *like a wildcat.*)

LARRY

Take your hands off her!

(*Taking* BOB *by surprise with his agility and sudden strength he throws* BOB *to the floor and gets on top of him.* JEANIE *runs to the door and bangs on it.*)

ME AND JULIET

JEANIE

Help, somebody! Help!

(BOB *grabs* LARRY'S *wrists and pulls his hands away easily and slowly, showing how much stronger he is.*)

BOB

What the hell do you think you're doing? (*He swings* LARRY *off his chest, still holding on to his wrists*) Want to fight, do you?

(*He throws* LARRY *on the couch.* RUBY *unlocks the door and comes running in.* BOB *is swinging back to slug* LARRY *and* RUBY *gets hold of his hand.*)

RUBY

Let him go, Bob! Get out of here!

(BOB *slings* RUBY *across the room.* LARRY *rises and jumps on top of* BOB's *back.* BOB *swings him around. They knock down a pile of mail-order boxes and the mail is scattered all over the floor.* MAC *comes to about this time and rejoins the free-for-all.* JEANIE, MAC, RUBY *and* LARRY *all hang on to* BOB, *who drags them around the room trying to break loose from them.* BETTY, *in her stage costume, comes running down the alley, peers through the window, sees what's up and joins the fight, jumping down onto the sofa and hanging on to one of* BOB's *legs. She is thrown over against the wall near the safe.* MAC *lands near her.* JEANIE *is thrown aside and* BOB *crashes down on the sofa on top of* LARRY. *They both lie still there for a moment, then* LARRY *starts to squirm slowly from underneath.* BOB's *arms and legs are limp. He is apparently knocked out.* LARRY *gets up and turns on the light.* JEANIE *runs to him.* RUBY *is the first to go over and take a look at* BOB.)

His head hit the radiator.

BETTY

(Out of breath)

Is he dead, I hope?

RUBY

No. But he's out—good and out!
(BOB's *five assailants are draped around the room, on chairs, on the desk, on the floor among the scattered mail-order envelopes—five breathless, panting, worn-out people, their clothes disheveled, their hair mussed. They lie and sit and lean in silence for a few minutes.* MAC *is lying with his head on* BETTY's *shoulder, her arm around him. Slowly he looks up at her and realizes whose arm is around him. He leaps back as if he had been bitten by a rattler, jumps to his feet, goes over to the loud-speaker and turns it off.*)

MAC

Next to last scene!

LARRY

Mac! We've got a lot of cues coming up!

BETTY

Gosh, I've got to make a change.

JEANIE

Me too.
(*Both exit.*)

MAC

You go back and take over. I'll stay here with Ruby.

LARRY

But . . .

MAC

Go ahead!

LARRY

Sure.
(LARRY *exits.* RUBY *closes the door.* MAC *fills a lily cup from the ice cooler, walks over and pours it on* BOB's *head.* BOB *groans, half awakened.* MAC *turns* BOB *over. There is a bruise on his head where it hit the radiator.* BOB *sits up slowly.* MAC *and* RUBY *stand still, watching him.* RUBY *goes to his desk, takes out a bottle of Bromo Seltzer, and pours some into a lily cup.*)

BOB

(*In a dull, bewildered voice*)
Last thing I remember is having my hands on his throat.
(*His eyes open wider. Fear crosses his face*) Did I kill him?

(RUBY *and* MAC *look at each other quickly. Then* MAC *lowers his head as if he were silently assenting that* BOB *killed* LARRY. RUBY *follows suit. He looks down too.* BOB, *now completely awakened by sudden fear, turns to the window and starts to climb out, then ducks his head back quickly*) There's a cop at the head of the alley.

RUBY

(*Surprised and happy to hear it*)
There is?

MAC

(*Quickly*)
Of course there is. I phoned for a cop an hour ago.

BOB

All right. I'll take what's coming to me. (RUBY, *having filled the lily cup with water, passes the Bromo Seltzer to* BOB. BOB *drinks it*) I couldn't help what I did. That little sneak stole my girl.

MAC

Girls don't get stolen, Bob. Watches get stolen. Money gets stolen. Girls don't get stolen. They go.
(BOB *sits on the sofa thinking it over.*)

MAC

(*Quietly*)
Suppose I could get you off?

BOB

How do you mean, get me off? Who are you, the Governor or somebody?

MAC

Suppose you had another chance. What would you do?

BOB

What the hell's the difference what I'd do?

MAC

You *have* got another chance, Bob. (BOB *looks from* RUBY *to* MAC) You didn't kill Larry.

BOB

(*Looking at* RUBY)

Is that right?

RUBY

He knocked you out.
(BOB *looks incredulous.*)

MAC

Well, he had a little help. The radiator back there.

BOB

(*Feeling his head*)

Where is he now? Did he go backstage?
(*He starts for the door.*)

ME AND JULIET

RUBY

They're *married,* you know.
(*Both* BOB *and* MAC *turn quickly toward* RUBY.)

MAC

Jeanie and Larry?
(RUBY *nods.*)

BOB

How do you know? When?

RUBY

Today. They needed a witness down at City Hall. I was it.

BOB

(*Grimly, to himself*)
How do you like that?
(*He goes over to the couch and sits down heavily.*)

RUBY

If you really mean that question, I like it fine. I think they'll do all right together.

BOB

(*As if he hadn't heard him*)
How do you like that?

MAC

He already told you.
(BOB *looks at* MAC. MAC *looks him straight in the eye.*
BOB *starts for the door.*)

MAC

Where are you going?

BOB

None of your damn business.
(*He goes out.*)

RUBY

He may be going backstage.

MAC

I'll get there first!
(*He climbs on the sofa and goes through the window.*
RUBY *is about to leave through the door when the
phone rings.* RUBY *runs back and picks up the phone.*)

RUBY

Hello! (*Into the phone*) Oh, hello, Mr. Harrison . . .
Really? (*His face lights up*) Maybe I can get him right now.
He just left this minute. Just a minute. (*He runs to the window and calls out*) Hey, Mac! Mac! (*He peers down the
alley and then goes back to the phone*) I was too late to get
him, but I'll go right back and tell him. You're going to trans-
fer him to the new show. Boy! Will he be tickled to death to

hear this news! (*The set is now receding upstage and the lights are coming down*) Tonight? Why—er—everything was fine tonight. Yes, the show went very smoothly. Not a hitch, Mr. Harrison. Not a hitch.

(*The lights fade as the set continues to move upstage.*)

SCENE V

The Orchestra Pit.

As the lights go out on Scene IV, the show curtain comes down and DARIO *is spotted in the pit, conducting change music into the last scene of* Me and Juliet. *It is a different* DARIO *now. As he conducts he looks angrily around at the lady of the gardenia, to see if she happens to be there, and he holds his lapel out to show her that he now wears a red carnation. He turns around and continues to conduct the change music, and the lights come up behind the curtain, which is transparent.*

Scene VI

Through the transparency the company is seen rushing into places, and the stagehands are just finishing setting the scene. LARRY *stands in the center, making sure that the scene is set before he gives the cue to ring up.* MAC *runs on.*

MAC

(To LARRY *in a loud whisper)*
Did Bob come back here?

LARRY

I haven't seen him. (MAC *joins* BETTY *and* JEANIE. LARRY *shouts to a carpenter)* Hey, Pete! Your third border is fouling that balcony piece!
(He goes upstage to supervise the adjustment.)

RUBY

(Running on)
Mac! I've got news for you! Mr. Harrison just called up. He's putting you in his new show!

MAC

Where's Betty? Baby, we're not in the same show any more . . . you know what that means?

138

No. Show me!
(She opens her arms. MAC *moves in.)*

LARRY

Places everybody—places! *(He runs across the stage)*
Everybody clear! *(He runs off, calling off stage to curtain man)* Take it up! *(But* MAC *and* BETTY *are still in an ecstatic embrace.* LARRY *shouts out to him, hoarsely)* Mac!
*(*MAC *is caught on stage as the curtain rises. Nimbly and ingeniously, he dodges behind one girl, then behind a boy and girl, and knowing the dance routine well, does his best to keep masking himself until he is near the exit and is able to slink off the stage. At the end of the refrain which is apparently the finale of* Me and Juliet *the curtain comes down, but the lights immediately come up again behind the transparent curtain, bringing us into the next scene.)*

Scene VII

The COMPANY *is breaking up just as it does after a finale. The stagehands immediately start to strike the set and the backdrop comes away.* LARRY *runs onto the stage as soon as the curtain has hit the floor.*

LARRY

Stand by, everybody! Don't take off your costumes.

GEORGE

(*Coming on from left*)
Keep your costumes on!
(*Everyone stops wherever he is and listens.*)

LARRY

I want to run the beginning of the first-act finale. (*Murmurs of protest from the* COMPANY) If we stay for five minutes now it will save us calling rehearsal tomorrow. (*Shouting across the stage*) Lily, get over there and sing "No Other Love."

A GIRL

I saw Lily dashing out of the theatre as soon as the curtain hit the floor.

ME AND JULIET

ANOTHER GIRL

She's singing over at Madison Square Garden.

LARRY

Oh, yes. That benefit. I forgot . . . Jeanie! Stand in for Lily, will you dear? (JEANIE *runs over to extreme right*) Take it from the second half! (*He indicates a vamp*) Go!

JEANIE

Hurry home, come home to me,
Set me free—
(BOB *enters, pauses, then crosses slowly in front of* JEANIE)
Free from doubt
And free from longing—
(JEANIE's *voice dies off, her throat tightening with fear.* LARRY *turns and sees* BOB's *scowling face and bulky figure lurching slowly toward him. He swallows hard, stands his ground and suddenly hears himself saying just what he ought to say.*)

LARRY

Bob, I've made a ten-o'clock call for tomorrow morning for you and Sidney. All the lights on the bridge have to be re-angled. So you and Sidney be here at ten o'clock . . .
(BOB *hesitates for a moment, then advances on* LARRY *as the company watch, tense and fearful of what* BOB *might do. As he comes up close to* LARRY *he stops and mumbles one line.*)

141

BOB

I didn't know you were married.
(*Pause.*)

SIDNEY

Ten o'clock. Okay, Bob?

BOB

(*Going past* LARRY)
I'll be here, I guess.
(*He exits with* SIDNEY. JEANIE'S *friends, having just heard the news that she has been married, start to cluster around her.* LARRY *shouts over to them.*)

LARRY

Hold it! (*They return to their places*) Take it from the last eight. (*He brings his arms up to indicate upbeat*) And . . .

JEANIE	LARRY
(*Singing right at* LARRY, *who doesn't look her way, but watches his company*)	
Into your arms I'll fly,	Bend way back, arms high.
Locked in your arms I'll stay,	Now travel, travel all the
Waiting to hear you say,	way around to your proper
No other love have I,	places . . .
No other love.	Watch your spacing.

THE CURTAIN FALLS